The Know-Nothing Campaign Against Higher Learning

The Know-Nothing Campaign Against Higher Learning

James Chandler

Prickly Paradigm Press, LLC

5751 S. Woodlawn Ave.

Chicago, IL 60637

www.prickly-paradigm.com

ISBN: 978-1-958846-18-6

Library of Congress Control Number: 2026944764

Printed in the United States of America on acid-free paper.

Contents

Contents

Preface

It was not until I woke up on the morning of Wednesday, November 6, 2024, that I received the news of Donald Trump's election to a second term. I was in London at the time to teach in the University of Chicago's Study Abroad program, including a course on "the age of democratic revolutions" in Europe and America from the 1640s through the 1830s. The last book we read was Alexis de Tocqueville's *Democracy in America*, with its trenchant analysis of unbridled populism under then-President Andrew Jackson and admonition that, for all its promise, the country stood in need of a system of advanced education. The eloquent liberalism of Tocqueville's writings about Jacksonian America could hardly fail to resonate this past year as I bore witness to an order of things under attack for being, precisely, "liberal"—the term having long since become, in certain quarters, a common slur.

When I returned home in late March, I confronted what a colleague called "the burning wreckage of American democracy" and, more particularly, what Trump—with the help of his soon-to-be abolished Department of Education—was already doing to universities. Claiming Title VI violations, the federal government had begun threatening them with the loss of federal funding, but without following the relevant Title VI procedures. I didn't understand why, collectively and individually, universities wouldn't defend themselves on both legal and academic grounds. Law firms and media networks were also, mystifyingly, caving without a fight. And corporate leaders and cabinet members, foreign leaders and international sports moguls, would soon be prostrating themselves, sometimes preemptively, to this president's insatiable need for fawning and flattery. But back in early April 2025, when—with the notable exceptions of Harvard, Princeton, and Wesleyan—no American university had risen to defend itself against an onslaught of questionable legality, I was dumbfounded. What was going on?

I soon recognized a dark irony of our situation: The current attempt to take over the universities was both raising the specter of the German 1930s and simultaneously masking itself as a campaign against antisemitism. I published an essay detailing the recent history of the issue as I saw it, going back to the rampant antisemitism of the 2017 "Unite the Right" rally in Charlottesville, Virginia (and Trump's response to it) and to the aftermath of the Hamas attack on Israel in October 2023. Even before this piece appeared in the *Los Angeles Review of Books* (June 6, 2025), I realized that my general take was already becoming widely shared, especially in the American Jewish protest movement "Not in Our Name," which had begun that spring to take to the streets and campuses.

Still, it seemed worthwhile to offer a factual account of a deeply implausible scenario, a narrative not just about Trump and his people crusading against antisemitism but also about the mainstream media's seeming acceptance of the ploy at face value. I followed this story up with another piece in the *LARB* (July 9), about the strange entanglements of the Trump administration and the "kayfabe" world of professional wrestling, with its distinctive ways of blurring realities. It centered on former World Wrestling Entertainment President Linda McMahon, now Trump's Secretary of Education, and her recent posturing in that role toward institutions like Harvard. The dark irony at the center of this second piece resides in the absurdity that such a person should be making any decisions whatsoever about American education—and McMahon was not the most egregiously outrageous of Trump's cabinet picks. At this point, I decided to build on these essays for a pamphlet about what I call the "new Know-Nothing" movement and its increasingly bold crusade against higher learning in America.

The first Know-Nothing movement, in the early 1850s, was pivotal for the history of American party politics. Its story provided a helpful frame, not least because certain powerful figures behind Trump, like former White House chief strategist Steve Bannon, have explicitly invoked the first Know-Nothings. Bannon has of course long pressed for "America First" anti-immigration policies under a far-right "brand" that also seems to challenge learning as such—though his weirdly ironized identification with what he calls "Know-Nothing vulgarians" comes partly from his illiberal understanding of American history itself. Strange ironies abound as well in the early history of the Know-Nothings: by the 1870s, their American Party had long since disbanded, but its legacy lived on as oppressed Irish and German Catholic immigrants became oppressors of others in their turn. Celebrated cartoonist Thomas Nast wickedly lampooned that development. The record shows, in other words, that the grand hypocrisies of these immigrants' descendants, Bannon and Trump, are by no means unprecedented.

"Higher learning"—a major target of the new Know-Nothing movement—might call for a gloss. A little more than a quarter-century ago, the esteemed Chicago anthropologist Marshall Sahlins, founder of this pamphlet press, recruited me for a special commission he had instigated, in the midst of a policy crisis at that university, to reflect on its mission and its future. Within this commission, three of us—Sahlins, historian William Sewell, and I—formed a little research group on higher education in the modern world. One of the texts we read and discussed was *The Higher Learning in America*, a 1936 publication by thirty-seven-year-old Robert Maynard Hutchins, who by then had already been president of the University of Chicago for eight years. Hutchins's book advocated for the *private* American research university, at a time when he judged many public universities to be too badly funded to fulfill their missions, especially with America's most gifted students. But as Sahlins was quick to remind us, Hutchins borrowed the title of this book from one of the earliest and most trenchant critics of the American university, Thorstein Veblen, also a former member of the Chicago faculty. Still republished and discussed to this day, Veblen's assessment was explicitly grounded in firsthand observation of the University of Chicago under its inaugural president, W. R. Harper. Veblen offered a precocious critique of what we now think of as the neoliberal effort to corporatize higher education, both private and public, with students understood as economic assets rather than moral or political subjects.

I have taught at the University of Chicago for nearly a half century, and, at least in certain moments, have accepted its proud self-understanding as the embodiment of the American research university—a claim that rests in part on its commitment to preserving, as many such institutions do in this country, a liberal arts college as its undergraduate "core." In *The Great American Research University* (2009), sociologist (and former Columbia provost) Jonathan Cole actually singled out Chicago as its ideal type, but one doesn't need to go that far to accept that it has long been a place where the very idea of "higher learning" has been both actively embraced and hotly contested.

The contemporary American university clearly had its share of critics before Trump came along. From the right, the culture war salvos of Allan Bloom and Dinesh D'Souza and the pro-Israel lobbying efforts of Daniel Pipes took aim at a range of targets, from hate-speech codes to Afrocentric curricula, deconstructionist literary criticism, and "political correctness."

From the left, the renewed Veblenian critique about the corporatization of the university has grown more intense than ever: This past year's reporting on higher education has cast the University of Chicago as a notable casualty of this trend. Marshall Sahlins could not save Chicago from falling prey to the dangers he foresaw, including those resulting from overspending. Even more than many other universities, it is now (literally) paying the price—and suffering reputational damage in the bargain.

To be clear, then, in exposing the motives and tactics of the Trump administration's campaign against higher learning and its liberal foundations, I don't deny the problems that plague today's universities or downplay the contestations that animate the current debates about higher education. I do maintain that these attacks, prosecuted in such bad faith, form no part of the solution to these problems. Instead, they represent an unprecedented threat to the core values and virtues that constitute the modern university's best hope and highest promise. A central goal of this pamphlet is to make these tactics, and the motives behind them, better understood.

One form of understanding that I offer here is simply journalistic, sorting the news in a time of rampant misinformation and deliberate efforts to "flood the zone." By academic training, however, I am a critic and cultural historian. So I have relied on my training as a critic to engage situations marked by ironies so dark that satire itself seems at once indispensable and impossible. But I have also relied on my training as a cultural historian. The five sections of this pamphlet each attempt to come to terms with a particularly urgent threat to our institutions of knowledge, including education at all levels in addition to public media, museums, and libraries. By placing those threats in broader historical contexts, I seek to make them legible as part of the current campaign—launched by Steve Bannon and his friend and fellow conservative activist David Bossie but sustained by their successors in the Trump administration—to Make America Know-Nothing Again.

These historical contexts are ranged along different scales. Some are relatively recent, such as the Trump administration's relation to antisemitism and its connections to the norms and practices of professional wrestling. Others reach back many centuries, to the long tradition of political satire and its distinctive ways of knowing and showing. It is the always-crucial middle distance of history, represented by the mid-nineteenth-century Know-Nothing movement, that returns as the relevant context for the last section of this pamphlet, where I consider the emergence of the modern American university in relation to the classical liberalism of Tocqueville and his friend John Stuart Mill.

In the 1830s, these two thinkers had already begun to address the seeds of tyranny in populist rhetoric during the presidency of Trump's hero Jackson, fully two decades before the Know-Nothing movement found its moment. I remain convinced that the best version of the modern American university, now under such unprecedented attack, is a fulfillment of Mill's early liberal hope to reconstitute institutional authority toward the end of that long "age of revolutions" on the dual foundation of principled discussion and scientific method. But I also follow UC Berkeley political theorist Wendy Brown in distinguishing this classical liberal university, especially in its public form, from a new version that began to have its values hollowed out by *neo*liberalism long before Trump and Bannon and McMahon came along. Brown's critique, which dates to a decade ago, itself looks back on the 1960s as higher education's heyday.

I began with a mention of my teaching in Chicago's Study Abroad program. I want to end by rejecting any suggestion that such an experience turns the students who share it into "elitist globalists" or counts on students who already are. Study abroad may still, alas, be considered a relatively privileged experience in expanding intellectual horizons, but what matters most in it is inseparable from a sound curriculum in liberal education. One three-hour class in my democracies course was given over to the students' reenactments of the various positions in one of the earliest debates about democracy in the Anglophone world, carried out by members of Oliver Cromwell's army after his defeat of the Royalist forces and the capture of King Charles I in 1647. The victorious army stopped at Putney on the outskirts of London and, for three days in St. Mary's Church on the south bank of the Thames, aired the arguments of those early modern democrats called the Levellers, radical Puritans whose parents had not gone to America in 1620 but stayed behind to fight their battles at home.

How should modern political representation be structured after the defeat of Royalism? What should be the fate of a king in an aspiring republic? Was owning property an appropriate basis for electoral participation? I assigned students to teams representing various roles in the debate irrespective of their varied socioeconomic backgrounds and ideological proclivities. Some left-leaning students argued the republican (lowercase) position on grounding the right to vote in property. Some right-leaning students argued the Levellers' case for universal franchise. After the morning's class in Central London, we took the Tube out to the church in Putney to be in "the room where it happened." Once there, the students began to play their morning roles all over again, spontaneously speechifying to one another. In the intellectual space of the classroom, and again in the historic space of St. Mary's church, they were opening up new vistas on their previously settled views—historical, geographical, and ideological—and of course on the lives they'd soon return to back in America.

This kind of horizon expansion is one of the greatest benefits of the modern liberal arts, as Tocqueville and Mill were among the first to see. For democracies to succeed, such benefits must be pursued with zeal and made available to ever-widening citizen cohorts. The problem is not that this experience, at home and abroad, is available to too many students, as the illiberal antiglobalists insist. The problem is that it is available to too few. Would it cost a lot of money—public and private—to scale it up for broader participation? Yes, an educated citizenry is an expensive proposition. But what better cause to spend the money on—another energy-guzzling AI data center? A new fleet of jets for ICE deportations? A $400 million gilded ballroom for our royal family?

Chicago, January 20, 2026

Introduction: The Spirit of a Dark Age

> "I can tell you one thing after going all over the world. History is on our side. The globalists have no answers to freedom."
>
> —Steve Bannon to Errol Morris, *American Dharma* (2018)

> "Who was so wild ... [to think] that a party unheard of ... with a self-chosen cognomen as ridiculous as satire itself could invent ... would suddenly spring up ... [and] absorb the elective strength of the state ... ?"
>
> —William Lloyd Garrison, *The Liberator*, 1854

Looking back from the end of the first year of Donald Trump's second term in office, one can easily lose sight of how important Steve Bannon has been in giving shape and purpose to the Trump presidency. Bannon, a former Goldman Sachs investment banker and Hollywood film producer, cofounded

Breitbart News as "the platform for the alt-right" in 2007, some years before the two men first met. His relationship with Trump over the past decade has been uneven, especially in respect to Trump's erratic moves in foreign policy—never more so than with the attack on Venezuela. Bannon has also become increasingly outspoken about his own agenda, and his recruitment of Trump to it, in ways that have required some public distancing on Trump's part. In late 2017, Trump fired Bannon as chief strategist at the White House, and there was a further public break in early 2018, when Bannon's critical comments about Trump and his children were published in Michael Wolff's *Fire and Fury*. Nevertheless, there can be little question that Bannon supplied an aggressively ideological program for a transactional candidate who notoriously lacked one. Nor that, having become Trump's "base," the MAGA movement under Bannon's leadership would push an agenda that included an attack on liberal institutions, especially American universities. The attack only grew bolder between Trump's first and second terms in office.

One pivotal moment came in August 2016, when Bannon replaced Paul Manafort as Trump's chief campaign strategist, though Bannon did not act alone in exerting such a mighty influence over the shape of things to come. A couple of weeks later, Bannon persuaded Trump to invite conservative activist David Bossie to join the team. Bossie, a longtime foe of Bill and Hillary Clinton, was the president of Citizens United, the organization responsible for the major deregulation of campaign financing in 2010 that helped set the stage for the current era in American politics. Bossie had earlier been party to the scheme to create the Willie Horton ads for George H. W. Bush's successful 1988 election campaign, but Bush later filed a formal complaint against Bossie for producing "the kind of sleaze that diminishes the political process." On October 7, 2016, a few weeks after Bossie joined Trump's campaign, *The Washington Post* released the notorious *Access Hollywood* tape with its recording of Trump's obscene boast about having his way with women.

Bannon and Bossie now had Trump where they wanted him. Trump needed to change the subject and up the stakes, as he has done many times since, not least in his protracted efforts to distract attention from the public outcry about the Jeffrey Epstein files. Less than a week after the release of the *Access Hollywood* tape, at a rally not far from his home base in Mar-a-Lago, Trump sounded the alarm about a vast international network of bankers whose ambition was nothing less than "to plot the destruction of U.S. sovereignty." Shockingly, three weeks later—with the benefit of some questionable campaign tactics and a little late help from FBI Director James Comey—Trump won the presidential election, with Bannon and Bossie now very much in charge of his political agenda.

A partial explanation for this turn of events lies in a story that Bannon likes to tell about his early days with Trump, for by 2016, he and Bossie and Trump already had some shared history. Bannon's story goes back to 2010, the year of the Citizens United decision, when Bannon and Bossie quickly formulated a plan for a wholesale renunciation of "globalism," the now-familiar term of abuse for an ideological bogey man that, since the fall of the Berlin Wall, has come to replace international communism as a terrifying worldwide menace in the eyes of the far right. Other terms are sometimes joined to "globalists" to form disparaging epithets—"far-left globalists" or even "far-left globalist elites"—but they all amount to so many redundancies. As Bannon would later recount, his updated "America First" campaign involved three key elements: restricting trade, closing borders, and avoiding "forever wars." But these three aspects of America's relationship with the wider world—involving (respectively) commerce, immigration, and military policy—were bound up with key elements in a parallel campaign to transform American domestic policy.

Linked to the three-part mission to remake the place of the United States in the world was a further mission to intimidate, attack, and transform American institutions deemed to be implicated in the nefarious work of far-left globalist elites. All three branches of government would have to be controlled. The American legal establishment would have to be cowed. And, crucially, independent sources of information and knowledge production—media outlets and universities—would have to be replaced or brought to heel. The goal of this last part of the domestic agenda was nothing less than a revolution in thought. How to tell if news is real or fake, what counts as science, what it means to be educated—these would all become questions newly up for grabs. As the campaign has unfolded, the links between the domestic transformation and Bannon's founding project have become ever clearer. Why push through the July 2025 rescission bill to remove funds already approved for NPR, PBS, and USAID? Mary Miller, MAGA member of Congress from downstate Illinois, explained her vote this way: "The days of Democrats' taxpayer-funded propaganda and far-left global programs are OVER."

Bannon may have become more frank in recent years about his ambitions, at some cost to his public relationship with Trump, but a decade and a half ago he clearly understood that he and

Bossie could succeed only if they remained mostly behind the scenes. Only after Trump gained office did Bannon go public with his account of how he and Bossie came to identify a real-estate developer turned reality-TV celebrity as the perfect vehicle for advancing their ambitious scheme. He has explained that in 2012, the year after Trump had spoken at the Conservative Political Action Conference (CPAC) (and began spreading rumors about President Obama's birth certificate), he and Bossie met with Trump in Trump Tower. At one point, Bannon called himself "a populist," a term Trump embraced (but repeatedly misheard as "a popularist"), and by the end of the meeting Bannon was telling himself that he might have found the front man for his great crusade. The cultivation of Donald Trump for this role had gone on privately for several years when, in November 2015, Bannon took their conversations public on Breitbart News. Hosting, and playing a wheedling "Steve" to his guest's "Mr. Trump," Bannon coached the presidential hopeful through a series of interviews on a range of subjects from China and Iran to oil and climate change. Anticipating the recent moves in Venezuela, Trump told Bannon in that November 19 broadcast that the United States should be seizing oil around the world. We needed, he said, to "take it out and keep it."

Trump and Bannon seem not yet to be on quite the same page in these interviews when it comes to so-called intellectual elites. In their first interview (November 5) they quibble about Bannon's sarcastic reference to "smart Republicans"—Trump, failing to hear Bannon's sarcasm, retorts that they are not smart but he (Trump) is. He even volunteers that he is keen to find a way to hold on to foreign students who "do great" at our best universities. One exchange in this broadcast stands out in Bannon's later telling. As the talk turns, inevitably, to immigration, Bannon reports Trump as having said, "I still want people to come in. But I want them to go through the process." Implying that he himself did *not* want people to come in, Bannon quotes himself (accurately) as replying: "You got to remember, we're Breitbart. We're the know-nothing vulgarians. So we've always got to be to the right of you on this." There is something strikingly disingenuous in Bannon's representation of his position on immigration as mere public posturing or political lane filling, as if it were not actually the position he strongly held and still holds. But the further interest of this remark lies in how Bannon makes the connection between policy and questions of knowledge: his self-identification with know-nothing vulgarians.

Here too Bannon is winking. His phrase "know-nothing" is something of an inside reference to the aforementioned Know-Nothing movement of the early 1850s, which took official political shape in 1854 as the American Party. His 2015 comment to Trump is not Bannon's only invocation of this group and their ideological preoccupations. He has signaled more than once that he sees the Know-Nothing movement as an important point of orientation for his own massive ambitions, the full dimensions of which came dismayingly into focus in the first year of Trump's second term in office. That 1850s movement, for all its brevity, was perhaps the most influential incarnation of the now all-too-familiar idea of "America First," or what historians often call American Nativism.

It was not, however, the first expression of America First. There had been a brief moment of nativism in 1835, and another in 1844. Nor would it be the last. The 1920s saw a serious recurrence of what happened in the 1850s. "We have a great desire to be supremely American," wrote President Calvin Coolidge in 1924. But the Know-Nothing movement of the early 1850s would eventually be recognized as having marked, and indeed enabled, a major pivot in antebellum American history. It helped both to end the old Whig Party in 1854 and to create the new Republican Party in

1856. Abraham Lincoln would be the Republican nominee for president in 1860.

The Know-Nothing movement was initially launched as a secret society, the Order of the Star-Spangled Banner, in 1849, itself a successor to an earlier secret society called One United America, or OUA. The growth of this organization over its brief lifetime was nothing short of mind-boggling, from forty-three members to over a million between 1852 and 1854. The society extended to both the North and South of 1850s America, but it took a slightly different shape in each region. Common to both parts of the movement, however, was a fierce resistance to immigration targeted chiefly at the Irish and the Germans, and above all at the Catholicism that many of these newcomers to America brought with them.

In the decade from 1845 to 1855, more than a million people arrived from Ireland and an even larger number from Germany—ten times the immigration levels from these countries twenty years earlier. The new post-Famine waves of Irish immigrants were objectionable to some Americans in ways that earlier generations had not been—not only because of their numbers but also because they were more likely than ever to be Catholic. Compared with earlier arrivals from Ireland, these immigrants were less skilled and poorer, and included Gaelic speakers without English. In Northern cities they were seen as a cause of rising crime rates and a danger to employment opportunities for native-born Americans. "No Irish Need Apply" first appeared in a *New York Times* want ad in 1854. The Know-Nothings sought to combat the perceived threat, and their movement won so much support in its first year that it attracted myriad voters away from the old Whig Party and into the new American Party, albeit briefly.

Other issues figured in this ideological mix, especially in the North. One was the question of temperance, so the party tended to incorporate attacks on the drinking habits of the Irish and Germans, with their whiskey and their beer.

Fig. 1. John H. Gouter, Irish and Germans stealing elections, early 1850s. New York Public Library Research Collections.

More important was the issue of slavery. The American Party attracted former Whigs because the Whig Party was held responsible for two bills—highly unpopular in the North—aimed at appeasing the slaveholding South: the Fugitive Slave Act and the Kansas-Nebraska Act. It was evidently not inconsistent for evangelical and other Protestants from the North to detest Irish immigrants and oppose slavery at the same time.

For Lincoln, however, the case was otherwise. Writing to his friend Joshua Speed in 1855, he expressed his own views about the Know-Nothings in no uncertain terms:

> I am not a Know-Nothing. That is certain. How could I be? How can anyone who abhors the oppression of negroes, be in favor of degrading classes of white people? Our progress in degeneracy appears to me to be pretty rapid. As a nation, we begin by declaring that "all men are created equal." We now practically read it "all men are created equal, except negroes." When the Know-Nothings get control, it will read "all men are created equal, except negroes, and foreigners, and catholics [*sic*]." When it comes to this I should prefer emigrating to some country where they make no pretence of loving liberty—to Russia, for instance, where

> despotism can be taken pure, and without the base alloy of hypocracy [*sic*].

As things turned out, the American Party's opposition to slavery was both fainthearted and short-lived. The party nominated former President Millard Fillmore at its 1855 convention and then came undone when delegates from Southern states pushed through a proslavery platform unacceptable to delegates from the North. After the Supreme Court's 1857 Dred Scott decision refusing citizenship to people of Black African descent, most antislavery members of the American Party joined the Republican Party that Lincoln would soon be leading.

One glaring irony in Bannon's invocation of the Know-Nothing movement as background for his and Trump's crusade has to do with their respective ancestries. Trump is a descendent of German immigrants and Bannon a descendent of Irish-Catholic immigrants. Trump's grandfather, Friedrich, arrived in the United States from Bavaria in 1886 with just a suitcase. Bannon's great-grandfather, Lawrence Bannon came over from Ireland in 1850, squarely in the middle of the same post-Famine mass exodus that triggered the rise of the Know-Nothings. Bannon's great-grandfather himself would thus presumably have suffered some persecution in the 1855 heyday of the movement, when Know-Nothing candidates held 140 seats in the House and Know-Nothing mayors were elected in Chicago and major cities across the northeast.

Indeed, had the Know-Nothing movement triumphed more completely and more immediately, Bannon's great-grandfather would not have been able to enter the United States when he did, or perhaps ever—there would be no Steve Bannon from Richmond, Virginia, to recruit Trump as the political face of his plan to close American borders. Unsurprisingly, in his own time Bannon has run afoul of the Catholic Church for suggesting that American bishops' public support of Deferred Action for Childhood Arrivals (DACA)—the immigration policy extending citizenship to the "Dreamers"—was just a way of filling empty pews. On November 12, 2025, in response to the aggression of Trump's immigrant crackdown and the rhetoric that supports it, the American bishops issued a strong statement condemning "the vilification of immigrants," defending their contributions, and affirming that Catholic teaching "exhorts nations to recognize the fundamental dignity of all persons, including immigrants."

I distinctly remember first encountering the Know-Nothing movement in a U.S. history course offered at my Catholic high school. It was a matter of particular interest, and its name was amusing to the adolescent mind. But the movement of the 1850s was not initially conceived as a celebration of ignorance. The manifestos produced on behalf of Know-Nothingism stake their intellectual claim in home-grown American Protestantism. A strong evangelical strain informed the Know-Nothing constituency: a firm commitment to understanding the world through Holy Scripture and to ensuring that the King James Bible, and no other, would be taught in public schools. But the Bible itself had to be read, after all, and Know-Nothings did promote literacy.

Among the more bookish adherents of the cause was James Harper, the cofounder of the great New York publishing house, who was elected mayor of that city on the American Party ticket in 1855. J. & J. Harper made its early reputation (and fortune) on the back of a rabidly anti-Catholic, anti-immigration novel of 1836, Maria Monk's *Awful Disclosures*, about a young woman abused by nuns in a convent. This novel sold hundreds of thousands of copies and eventually earned a reputation as a nativist *Uncle Tom's Cabin*. Like Stowe's, the book offered itself as enlightened critique, not as deliberate obscurantism. The word "Enlightened" appears often in Know-Nothing writings of the 1850s.

The Know-Nothing label, historians speculate, may have derived not from the movement's resistance to enlightened understanding as such, but rather from responses given by members of the secret society who, when asked about their organization, were supposed to have said: "I know nothing." In a modern Irish context, this evokes the famous line in Seamus Heaney's poem about the IRA: "Whatever you say, say nothing." And yet it seems that the Know-Nothings, though they preferred to be identified with the American Party, themselves sometimes employed the seemingly unflattering epithet for their projects. As Tyler Abinder, the leading historian of the movement, has pointed out: "One of the first newspapers to support the new movement was entitled the Boston Know Nothing, and even in 1856, the organization continued to call its political yearbook the Know Nothing Almanac" (*Nativism and Slavery*, 14).

Richard Hofstadter noted in *The Age of Reform* (1955) that the Know-Nothing movement was "based almost entirely on conspiratorial ideology," and thus in a series of American political movements for which the through line was not so much ignorance and unreason as fear and hate. When Hofstadter returned to the Know-Nothings in *Anti-Intellectualism in American Life* (1963), he told the story this way:

> There has always been in our national experience a type of mind which elevates hatred to a kind of creed; for this mind, group hatreds take a place in politics similar to the

> class struggle in some other modern societies. Filled with obscure and ill-directed grievances and frustrations, with elaborate hallucinations about secrets and conspiracies, groups of malcontents have found scapegoats at various times in Masons or abolitionists, Catholics, Mormons, or Jews, Negroes or immigrants, the liquor interests or the international bankers. In the succession of scapegoats chosen by the followers of this tradition of Know-Nothingism, the intelligentsia have at last in our time found a place. (37)

Still, some historians do link Know-Nothingism with the populism that preceded it (Mark Voss-Hubbard, *Beyond Party*). This populism already had a recognizably anti-intellectual component in the early nineteenth century, as early liberals like Alexis de Tocqueville and John Stuart Mill pointed out at the time. I discuss some implications of Trump's turn to Jacksonian populism in section 5.

But why would the Know-Nothings embrace a term that sounds so much like a slur? Perhaps they were rejecting a certain *kind* of knowledge: cosmopolitan, global, and, of course, anything pertaining to the Roman Church. International Catholicism in the 1830s was the forerunner of the twentieth-century specter of international communism bent on global domination, and possibly also the twenty-first-century specter of Islam, which Bannon often singles out as another global threat to his notion of the American way of life. Certainly, Bannon's own references to the movement show that he is aware of the implications of the term "Know-Nothing" beyond the closing of ranks in a secret organization. He himself has made the connection between his own anti-immigration campaign and what one might call "the question of learning" with remarks like his 2012 comment to Trump about how the Breitbart team needs to represent itself publicly as "the know-nothing vulgarians." When Bannon first announced the launch of his daily talk show on Breitbart in November 2015, the very month he began featuring interviews with Trump, he declared that its programming was for "those 'low information' citizens who are mocked and ridiculed by their 'betters'—the clueless elites."

The scare quotes around "low information" might seem to suggest irony, but this is not the Socratic irony implicit in the philosopher's famous declaration that he knows nothing, the kind of irony that has long informed discussion in the liberal arts classroom. In explaining himself on this occasion, Bannon went on to flatter his audience as "the most hungry for news, information, and analysis on the web." Yet in his latest programming enterprise, the

Bannon's War Room podcast (launched in October 2019), all traces of an educational mission have fallen away, along with any pretense of journalism. In his July 1, 2024 interview with *The New York Times*'s David Brooks, Bannon explained: "I'm not a journalist. I'm not in the media. This is a military headquarters for a populist revolt. This is how we motivate people. This show is an activist show. If you watch this show, you're a foot soldier. We call it the Army of the Awakened."

Bannon's representation of himself as a nonelite—in public posture and also, for instance, in his mode of dress—can hardly be taken seriously considering his degrees from Harvard and Georgetown, his work at Goldman Sachs, and his time in Hollywood managing media mergers. Among his other ventures, he has profited greatly from *Seinfeld* reruns. But the implications of the military metaphors he now regularly deploys are clear enough. The time for knowledge—for "information" and "analysis"—seems to have passed. Foot soldiers don't ask questions. They take orders. Bannon, who calls his website "a killing machine," is their general, the leader of the new Know-Nothings.

Bannon is a nationalist who regularly boasts that he travels the world shoring up other countries' right-wing nationalist leaders: Viktor Orbán in Hungary, Marine Le Pen in France, Giorgia Meloni in Italy. But he does not identify his enemies in this so-called war in nationalist terms—Russia, say, or Iran, or China. No, the real enemies are those "clueless elites" whom Bannon contrasts with his own foot soldiers: the globalists, the Know-Somethings. Journalism itself—typically branded as the "left-wing," "mainstream" media—is one bastion of the Know-Somethings. But the citadel of the enemy realm, the institution that must be toppled, is the American university. This siege will be undertaken not in the name of enlightenment but in the name of an all-out war. The old right-wing challenge against universities—that professors and students were pursuing activism, not knowledge—has been turned on its head. Bannon makes no bones about it. Xenophobic America-First Know-Nothingism is sheer activism—and what Bannon calls his "war" is just activism by other means.

Today's Know-Nothingism comes in many forms, and accordingly, Trumpian authoritarianism serves plans and schemes beyond those of Bannon and ongoing Trump favorite Stephen Miller. These range from Project 2025 (produced by the Heritage Foundation) to the pilot takeover of education staged in Florida by Governor Ron DeSantis and conservative activist Christopher Rufo, and the many provocations of the Israel lobby, including its evangelical wing at the Esther Project. Not all these proponents emphasize exactly the same aspects of Know-Nothingism that animate Bannon's army. Nor are they all as open as Bannon about what they are up to and why. Bannon's forthrightness as a semi-outsider singles him out, and that is surely why he has become so popular on the interview circuit in recent years—not least in the extended conversations of Errol Morris's feature-length documentary, *American Dharma* (2018), a must-see for anyone seeking to come to terms with the spirit of our dark age.

Precisely because Bannon is so forthcoming about his ideas and ambitions, his contradictions are everywhere apparent. He is an avowed "economic nationalist" who claims to be taking action on behalf of people who have been left behind in recent decades. Yet he staked his movement on a billionaire whose tax policies have most benefited those in his (and Bannon's) own oligarchical circle. He is an avowed populist who declares he'd rather see the country governed by the first hundred people in MAGA hats to come through the door in a Trump rally than by the "scientific, engineering, and globalist elites" who have been in charge for too long. Yet he supports the authoritarianism of a president willing to call his most loyal followers "weaklings" if they ask the wrong questions, as they have done about the Epstein files.

Even more to the point, Bannon conceives his role in the movement as a leader who demands blind obedience from his "men." He might praise the wisdom of those he claims to have turned into a virtual community on his website, yet at the point of mobilization, which can never come too soon for him, all that matters is their whipped-up rage. Bannon will eagerly assert that "the key to these sites [like the *War Room*] was the comment section." But the comment section is not a curation of deliberated opinion aimed at the best possible judgment and course of action. The goal from the start was to see opinion "weaponized at some point in time," because the "angry voices, properly directed, have latent political power." The direction comes from General Bannon, who is not to be questioned—and who now boasts of having taken his antiglobalist campaign worldwide. On the day he reported to prison, July 1, 2024 (for four months, convicted of mail fraud and money laundering in the "We Build the Wall" fundraising campaign), Bannon told the BBC that he "was unconcerned about missing a crucial part of Trump's campaign, as there is a 'Maga army' ready to ensure the former president defeats Joe Biden."

In view of such ambitions and the conditions of politics and culture they demand, it is no surprise that in Trump's second term, even more aggressively than in his first, he and his team have relentlessly attacked the liberal—in the sense of deliberative—institutions of modern society: the free press, the rule of law, and the modern university. There is no place in an authoritarian world order imposed with rage and enforced through fear for the kind of open discussion and reflection that such institutions both depend on and promote. The resort to intimidation, especially in the second term, is precisely what has caused so many anxious observers to speak of an encroaching fascism in this country and to look for a precedent to Germany in the 1930s—or even America in the 1920s. One such observer is Yale-educated J. D. Vance, who in the lead-up to the 2016 election likened Trump to a second Hitler. But this was before he was persuaded that this second Hitler might help his political advancement. Nowadays he likes to claim—as he did in a speech at NatCon2 on November 10, 2021, and as many fascists have done over time—that "professors are the enemy."

Neo-Nazism came to the fore in the events of August 2017 in Charlottesville, and the first Trump administration was notoriously slow to condemn it. Bannon himself was initially reported to be a casualty of that episode, though Trump had apparently been contemplating his ouster earlier, after reports surfaced about Bannon taking credit for the election victory. Bannon has always protested that he is not a White nationalist, that his movement has no room for neo-Nazis–and that he is neither antisemitic, as his first wife alleged, nor a racist, as the Southern Legal Counsel charged. On other occasions, however, he has instructed his followers not only to accept epithets like "racist" and "nativist" but also to "wear them like a badge of honor." Most importantly, he does little to discourage the connection with the original Know-Nothings, and perhaps ultimately with the war they waged on Irish immigrants.

Besides nineteenth-century media mogul James Harper, another prominent member of the Know-Nothing party in the New York of the early 1850s was William "the Butcher" Poole, whose violence against Irish Catholics was memorably restaged on screen by Daniel Day-Lewis in Martin Scorsese's 2002 *Gangs of New York*. Perhaps even more than Harper, who was after all politic enough to become Mayor of New York, Poole represents an ironic nineteenth-century exemplar for Bannon's new Know-Nothingism. As the brutal leader of the Bowery Boys, he assumed the role of a gang lord hell-bent on blocking immigrants and extirpating Roman Catholic globalism. Though he left little by way of a written record, the *Brooklyn Eagle* for February 9, 1853 notes a William Poole elected to serve a three-year term in the sixth ward of New York City's Board of Education. This would make a degree of sense, since so many of the Know-Nothing movement's issues centered on the question of exactly what was being taught in schools. But if this was indeed *the* William Poole, as seems likely, he would have been responsible for shaping the educational experience of students in New York schools in the decade after the arrival of Lawrence Bannon from Ireland. I can find no information about whether Steve Bannon's great-grandfather came first to New York, like so many other famine immigrants did. But the thought of him under the tutelage of Daniel Day-Lewis's William Poole character in *Gangs of New York* is an image to reckon with.

Another Catholic immigrant of this moment, Thomas Nast, who definitely did attend New York City schools in the 1850s, would go on to become the greatest political cartoonist of his age. Nast was born in Bavaria in 1840 and came to the United States as part of the same Irish and German waves of immigration that the Know-Nothing movement was created to oppose. Nast's career was well advanced by 1870, when he produced a cartoon about how American attitudes to immigration were evolving. Once the Germans and Irish Catholics assimilated, many of them in their turn struck a hard-line anti-immigration stance toward new Chinese arrivals. Recognizing this irony led Nast to one of his most famous and prophetic satirical efforts:

"Throwing Down the Ladder by Which They Rose." Atop the newly walled border around the United States, under an updated Know-Nothing flag, stand assimilated Irish and German Catholic immigrants. They are led by President Patrick and Vice President Hans, presumably Irish and German leaders of the new Know-Nothings, a reincarnation of the very movement that had so relentlessly persecuted them, or their parents, a quarter of a century earlier.

THROWING DOWN THE LADDER BY WHICH THEY ROSE.

Fig. 2. Thomas Nast, "Throwing Down the Ladder by Which They Rose," *Harper's Weekly*, July 23, 1870. New York Public Library Digital Collections.

Nast was one contemporary who associated the Know-Nothing movement not just with xenophobia but also, taking the name at face value, with ignorance. Yet his satirist's instincts led him to a figure and a fact that has persisted over decades and perhaps never been more resonant than today. It is hard to look at this 1870 cartoon without thinking of the Irish-American president of *Breitbart News* and the German-American president of the United States. More is involved here than mere policy. Beyond reviving the same kind of Know-Nothing immigration proposals that would have kept their own ancestors out of this country, Steve Bannon and Donald Trump have also supported their effort with the same kind of illiberal xenophobic rhetoric that the nineteenth-century Know-Nothing movement used to stoke that first campaign.

Nast's cartoon represents a case of "situational irony," understood as a certain turn or "twist" of events in which circumstances invert what we might reasonably have expected: the fire in the fire station. Situational ironies abound in our dark moment, and each of the sections that follows attends to at least one of them: a neofascist takeover masked as a crusade against antisemitism in universities; a major player from the murky world of professional wrestling in charge of education policy; a government crackdown on major media outlets carried out in the name of free speech; a narcissistic president who governs by greed and whimsy touted as a strategic genius; a thought that we might do without the combined advantages of liberal education and the research university that have, ever since Tocqueville's and Mill's liberal critiques of Jacksonian America, constituted a principal source of American strength.

But another way irony matters here lies not so much in circumstances as in our response to them. This is irony as trope or device, a discursive twist of tone or implication often associated with the genre of satire. In addition to identifying situational ironies, I look at ironic responses to them in satirical practice across media. Following the insightful offbeat Irish commentator Blindboy Boatclub, however, I also show how Trump and his team have attempted to use Know-Nothing tactics to inoculate themselves against the effects of satire—not least in adopting the modus operandi of that world of professional wrestling in which not only our Secretary of Education but also the President himself have been such prominent figures over the years. Linda McMahon was cofounder of World Wrestling Entertainment, along with her husband, Vince (since indicted for distributing steroids to his wrestlers), and Trump is an official member of its Hall of Fame.

The WWE is not to be confused with the UFC (Ultimate Fighting Championship), the martial arts group Trump hosted for a series of bouts on the White House Lawn as part of the country's 250th anniversary celebrations in 2026. Trump would of course prefer to cast himself as a martial arts combatant, but he is better understood as a performer in the pre-scripted drama of the wrestling ring, where egregious buffoonery mixes the roles of the hero and the "heel." The result is a world governed by the conventions of "kayfabe," a way of blending illusion and reality, the playful and the serious, that the great French critic Roland Barthes has accurately described as offering "a spectacle without thought." Kayfabe might be considered the antithesis of what the philosopher Richard Rorty has called "liberal irony," a Socratic capacity to look at a situation from many thoughtful perspectives at the same time—not to be confused with the deeper existential condition that the late Jonathan Lear found in Kierkegaard's version of Socratic irony. Kayfabe asks that we accept the spectacle offered without having any thoughtful perspective at all, a demand that makes it the perfect expression of the new Know-Nothing movement.

Bearing in mind, then, that satire has become a particularly crucial response to illiberal unknowing in our time, I will leave the final word on Bannon and his immigrant great-grandfather to the brilliant comedian Trevor Noah, himself an immigrant to America (from South Africa). After hearing

Bannon's criticisms of DACA in a *60 Minutes* interview back in 2017, Noah did a little research and learned the facts about Bannon's ancestry. Here is how he reported his findings to the September 12 audience of *The Daily Show*, a television program he succeeded Jon Stewart in hosting:

> Lawrence Bannon arrived in the U.S. from Ireland by the 1850s, at a time when America's borders were so open that Irishmen could walk into the country with no passports, no visas, no background checks of any kind. ... So in many ways, Steve Bannon's great-grandfather was a DREAMer.
>
> Yeah, and his great-grandson is a f***ing nightmare.

1
A "Total Assault" on Universities

Fig. 3. Screenshot of documentary footage from the "Unite the Right" rally, in Spike Lee's *BlacKKKlansman* (2018).

We all remember the assault on an American university in August 2017, when White nationalists without authorization marched menacingly across the Lawn of the University of Virginia, one of the nation's oldest and most respected institutions of higher learning. The events of that weekend were horrific, but at least they made a certain kind of sense. This was, after all, an attack supported by the

Ku Klux Klan on an elite university. Former Klan Grand Wizard David Duke himself was on hand in Charlottesville to explain that the lethal events there represented a "turning point" in the effort "to fulfill the promises of Donald Trump." Moreover, the spectacle of White supremacists with neo-Nazi paraphernalia chanting "Jews will not replace us" came as no surprise to anyone who knew the history of the Klan since its reemergence in 1915. Blacks and Jews alike had been targets of its depredations for over a century, and Blacks and Jews had joined hands in social justice movements to fight back.

It is an alliance that Spike Lee emphasized in *BlacKKKlansman* (2018), an improbable film based on a mostly factual memoir about a Black policeman's infiltration of the Klan in the 1970s. Lee pointedly adapted the book for his Oscar-winning screenplay to include a Jewish cop as the Black cop's co-conspirator, thus invoking the long-standing political solidarity between Blacks and Jews in this country. Indeed, Lee ends his film with a fantasy sequence that carries the audience from its Black protagonists' witnessing a white-robed Klansmen's cross-burning ceremony near Colorado College in the 1970s to the March in Charlottesville with its dreadful chant, "Jews will not replace us." During this sequence, Lee cuts away to footage of Donald Trump making his notorious claim, in response to the fatal encounter between the Klansmen and the peaceful protesters who opposed them, that there were "very fine people" on both sides. Two years later, during the first presidential debate with Joe Biden (September 29, 2020), Trump would issue a brazen message to the Proud Boys (a group identified by the Anti-Defamation League as both antisemitic and White supremacist) to "stand by" until needed—as they apparently were on January 6, when they too would be come to be seen as very fine people in his eyes.

The more recent attacks on American universities are far more threatening than the one in Charlottesville because they are both more sweeping and, at least initially, less intelligible. But the strategy became clearer in the spring of 2025, a year out from the widespread student protests against the devastation in Gaza. Columbia University President Minouche Shafik had been summoned to appear before Congress a year earlier, on April 17, 2024. In the early months of the second Trump administration, it was time to face a dismaying truth about the Trumpian crusade: a quasi-fascist assault on institutions of higher education was being cynically masked as a battle against antisemitism.

It was now, one would have thought, impossible not to see that the Trump administration has a domestic agenda with major ulterior goals—that they mean to target universities for perceived liberal leanings, to deport students on ideological grounds, to clamp down on sexual and gender freedoms, and to roll back the hard-won achievements of the civil rights movement. Christopher Rufo, one of the architects of the current assault on higher education, began to speak more explicitly about this last goal after scaling up his Florida work for Ron DeSantis to a national effort for Trump. One of the key points debated in Rufo's *New York Times* interview with the conservative op-ed writer Ross Douthat (March 7, 2025) was the cards-on-the-table question of whether the linchpin 1964 Civil Rights Act should be turned inside out or simply repealed outright.

An appalling irony had surfaced in the fact of a far-right takeover that was both enforced by authoritarian measures reminiscent of Germany in the 1930s and masked as a crusade against antisemitism. And astonishingly, Trump's rationale continued to be taken at face value even in the media outlets that he vilified as liberal or "sleazebag" (the terms are almost synonymous for him). Reporting in April 2025 on the freezing of $2.2 billion in research funding after Harvard refused to comply with the administration's sweeping demands, CNN, for example, could comment naïvely that "the proposed changes are the latest effort of the federal task force to combat antisemitism on college campuses after a spate of high-profile incidents around the country in response to the Israel–Hamas war in Gaza." Yet few of the more informed observers believed that the task force's targeting of Harvard—or Columbia, Brown, Cornell, and Northwestern—had much of anything to do with antisemitism. An important statement titled "Not in Our Name," signed by thousands of Jewish and Israeli faculty members across the country, made this point forcefully. Beyond the university, Not in Our Name began to take to the streets. Timothy Snyder at Yale and James Schamus, addressing fellow Jewish professors at Columbia, both argued publicly that the attacks on these universities are themselves antisemitic. Michael Roth, President of Wesleyan University, warned in an April 5 *New York Times* op-ed that "Trump is selling Jews a dangerous lie."

How did we come to such a pass? Much of the multipronged effort launched in the first months of Trump's second term, including the funding cuts for overhead costs in science grants to universities and the rollback of measures taken to advance the cause of civil rights in America, had already been outlined in the education section of the Heritage Foundation's Project 2025—a plan that Trump of course repeatedly disavowed in his run for reelection. Crucially, Project 2025, drafted well before the autumn of 2023, makes no mention of antisemitism in its proposed "reforms" of American education. (The Heritage Foundation's supplemental plan, Project Esther, does, but its quiet release did not occur until October 7, 2024, just a month before the election, a week after Trump's public message to the Proud Boys.)

A reasonable starting point for explaining how antisemitism came to be mobilized on behalf of such a reactionary and calculated campaign is the resignation of Liz Magill as President of the University of Pennsylvania in early December 2023. Her decision to step down came just days after her interrogation by Elise Stefanik, a Republican House member from New York, when she gave a legally correct answer to a carefully crafted trap question: "At Penn, does calling for the genocide of Jews violate Penn's rules or code of conduct?" The immediate occasion for congressional questioning of three university presidents, including Magill, was their universities' responses to the atrocities of the October 7 attack by Hamas on Israeli citizens. Yet Magill, who resigned first, was called to face congressional interrogation in no small part because of a controversy earlier that autumn in which she ran afoul of some of Penn's major donors.

Penn had hosted a literary festival in September 2023 by the organization Palestine Writes, which several of Penn's biggest funders, including Board Chair Marc Rowan, attempted to block. In response, Magill issued a statement condemning antisemitism on campus but also insisting that the festival should go forward as part of Penn's commitment to free expression. By December, the escalation from donor pressure to congressional pressure proved fatal to her presidency, as it would for Claudine Gay's presidency at Harvard. This same combination of congressional and donor pressure would later lead to the resignation of Columbia's President Shafik.

By the April 2024 congressional hearing, the death toll in Gaza had risen to over 30,000, with massive destruction of schools and hospitals, and protests initially launched in the late autumn. Columbia's protest had taken the form of an encampment on campus, and soon, partly in solidarity with Columbia's students, there would be hundreds of encampments on campuses across the country, involving tens of thousands of student protesters. As the war raged on, the presence of these encampments and the activities of the participants posed questions that were debated on campus and off. For these protesters, the point was to speak up in defense of a people being decimated in Gaza and brutally suppressed in the West Bank. For the vast majority, the targets were both the policies of an Israeli state under the problematic leadership of

Benjamin Netanyahu and the support of them with American tax dollars ($40 billion over the previous decade, much of it for armaments).

For some, the targets of the protest extended to the larger Zionist enterprise and its consequences for Palestinians since 1948. Many of those involved, students and faculty alike, were Jews; not a few were Israelis. To the extent that the protests targeted Israeli state policies, they raised questions (strange ones, perhaps) about whether objection to what the state of Israel is doing in Gaza could make a Jew, or anyone else, an antisemite. To the extent that the protests targeted Zionism itself, they raised further questions about the relationship between antisemitism and anti-Zionism. And, of course, to the extent that these were protests—speech that goes beyond routine discussion to address a situation of emergency or crisis—they raised questions about how much freedom the participants should be accorded.

The answers to all these questions were different in different settings. I remember an interview conducted by NPR's Ari Shapiro with two liberal Zionist journalists, Franklin Foer and Julia Ioffe, who had covered the question of antisemitism in recent years. At the time, in May 2024, I found it very unsatisfactory, and having recently listened to it again, I still do. The interlocutors danced awkwardly around the central question of what distinguishes

…isemitism, until at one point …en more awkward juxtaposition …wish students were experiencing …tests and the slaughter taking place

…HAPIRO: Frank, what do you think about the argument that the real trauma from past events and fear about what future events may bring should take a back seat to the ongoing killing of tens of thousands of Palestinians?

FOER: I would say it's not even just—I mean, I think that minimizes what Jews are experiencing on campuses and in the world just to say that it's an expression of past trauma, which—obviously it's filtered through past trauma [...] But if you—on college campuses and in neighborhoods and—there are these very real examples of antisemitism. And just because there's one crisis that's happening in Gaza does not mean that there are not other crises that are happening in the world.

This barely coherent response was more than a little troubling. I was listening to this broadcast with a friend in my car, and we both realized that further trouble lay ahead.

To questions about the latitude th given to student protest, answers also vari The denouement at Columbia was widely t as were events at UCLA. I happened to have the spring 2024 term at the University of Virg site of the deadly Klan march in 2017. There, early May, the state police were called in to clear small and peaceful protest near Jefferson's Rotunda; the state police had not been summoned against the White nationalists' march on the Lawn. At Northwestern, where the president had earlier in the protests discouraged the flying of Palestinian flags but not Israeli flags, the university administration eventually negotiated an agreement with protesting students. Hit in April 2025 with a $790 million threat from the Trump administration, the university seemed to be paying a price for that flexibility. (Northwestern's subsequent months-long battle to defend itself against the Trump administration's charges of antisemitism ended in late November with its agreement to a $75M penalty.)

At Chicago, there was a clear effort to find a way to end the encampments before the June commencement ceremony, which was to be staged on the central quadrangles where the protesters had pitched their tents. On returning from Virginia in May, I was told by a colleague that negotiations were taking place and that the student representatives had narrowed down their hopes to a single concession from the university—committed, as they knew it to be, to academic norms above all others. The request was that the university publicly acknowledge what a UN commission report released on April 18, 2024 had already determined: that "scholasticide" was taking place in Gaza. The state of Israel, the students are reported to have stipulated, need not have been named in any such statement. Whether this ever became the sole student demand is a matter of dispute, but there was a lot of faculty support for the students and for their shrewd proposal. I sent two letters myself to our president encouraging this concession but got no reply. Campus police eventually cleared the tents in the dark of night a few days before the commencement ceremony. At the ceremony itself, on June 8, several students walked out to protest the university's withholding the diplomas of four students involved with the encampment.

Since the crackdowns of spring 2024, universities have rewritten their codes of conduct to install draconian rules inhibiting or prohibiting protest, with dubious implications for the norms of free speech and academic freedom. None of this revented the unappeasable Trump administration making the campus events of 2024 the ostenunds for the unprecedented assault that inue to unfold throughout the first year of Trump's second term, despite the best efforts of many educators and journalists to expose its cynical hypocrisy.

By the end of Trump's first year in office, his polling numbers had been hit hard by controversy over the Epstein files, failure to control rising prices, and a series of foreign policy fiascos. Some cracks in the MAGA façade of concern about antisemitism had also begun to show. The surge of MAGA support for Nick Fuentes, outspoken neo-Nazi antisemite and Holocaust denier, aspiring heir to the late Charlie Kirk's political movement, caused untold problems for the agenda of the Heritage Foundation. The foundation landed in a quandary when Fox News host Tucker Carlson warmly welcomed Fuentes, and many of his 20 million America First Groyper followers, for a two-hour interview on his podcast. Unchallenged by Carlson, Fuentes waxed both nativist and Nazi about "organized Jewry" as a "transnational gang" threatening American unity, and there followed a public outcry. But Carlson is a friend and ally of Kevin Roberts, the head of the Heritage Foundation, and when Roberts defended him, major rifts on the right began to widen. In a sense, we have circled back to Charlottesville in 2017.

It matters enormously, through all this, that some of the observers most genuinely and sincerely concerned about incidents of antisemitism on American campuses are taking exception to the Trump administration's tactics. Many reject the idea that some conspiracy theory of left-wing antisemitic brainwashing is needed to explain why so many students have joined so much of the rest of the world in condemning the systematic devastation in Gaza. I've cited some disappointing coverage from the liberal mainstream media, so I will close on a more optimistic note.

As early as March 2025, NPR's *Morning Edition* aired an interview with Kenneth Stern, the Bard College professor and self-declared Zionist who had primary responsibility for drafting the International Holocaust Remembrance Alliance's working definition of antisemitism. The immediate occasion was the Trump administration's threat to withhold $400M to Columbia (this was before the announcement of threats against Brown, Cornell, Northwestern, and Harvard). Stern, who had already gone public in *The New Yorker* (March 13) with anxieties that his own definition was being adversely weaponized, was asked what he made of the administration's claim that "it is going to root out antisemitism specifically on college campuses [...] telling 60 colleges they're under investigation for failing to protect Jewish students." Here is his answer:

> I think it's a total assault on the university, which has been a very important institution, you know, for Jews over the last number of decades. J. D. Vance had talked about sort of following the playbook of Orbán in Hungary on dealing with education. And I think that's what we're seeing unfolding. We're seeing an attempt to not ... make a distinction between actual harassments, true threats and so forth [but rather] to go after the views of people and hurt the university that way.

Asked about the case of Mahmoud Khalil, the Algerian Palestinian graduate student from Columbia arrested and taken to a prison in Louisiana, Stern responded:

> And when you start saying that we're going to go after people whose speech we don't like—for nothing more—that's the predicate. Where does that end? To me, one of the things that's important for our ability to combat antisemitism and other forms of hate is having strong democratic institutions. When we're assaulting free speech, that's McCarthyism. We don't have strong democratic institutions anymore.

After emphatically declaring that the administration was "absolutely weaponizing antisemitism" and thus making Jewish students less safe rather than more so, Stern explained his larger approach to education:

> When I teach, and I teach about antisemitism and I teach about Israel and Palestine, I want students to be able to say what they think. I want to create a space where they feel comfortable to be wrong and experiment with ideas. If we don't have that as the core of the American educational enterprise, we're going to suffer tremendously in the long run.

It is worth listening to Stern's words in his own compelling voice, the voice of a committed Zionist who is also a committed educator at one of our newly vulnerable liberal arts colleges.

Kenneth Stern or Donald Trump—which one genuinely cares about the interests of Jewish students, and Jews more broadly? Whom should we trust when it comes to the sensitive and crucial issues of our moment—antisemitism, academic freedom, free speech, and the contested issues of liberal education in America, to say nothing of Gaza, where the rubble of devastation is now itself buried under the rubble of subsequent news cycles? These questions need to be posed again and again until this cynical campaign to take down our colleges and universities on bogus pretenses ceases to have even a shred of public credibility.

2
A "Spectacle Without Thought"

Fig. 4. Trish Stratus and then-WWE President Vince McMahon, with his wife, Linda McMahon, in the background, WWE *Smackdown* event, May 3, 2001. https://www.youtube.com/watch?v=zQ0bGm82q0k

In an escalation of both its attack on higher education and its crackdown on dissenting opinion in this country, the Trump administration announced in May 2025 that it was suspending interviews for international student visas until it had the capacity to screen applicants' social media for content it considered politically objectionable. After the process was restarted a month later, applicants were required to make their social media accounts public, and consular officers were instructed in the broadest of terms to look for "any indications of hostility toward the citizens, culture, government, institutions or founding principles of the United States." So the many foreign students who have expressed concerns about, say, U.S. support for the war in Gaza might well be out of luck.

Like so many such news items in the first year of Trump's second administration, this development was deeply troubling and yet sadly predictable. It was entirely in line not only with the administration's recent power moves but also with its not-so-subtle signals of what to expect next. Some of those moves had been made in the high-profile fight that the administration picked with Harvard University—and may be in violation of Title VI rules and the First Amendment principles they claim to be defending. Likewise, some of the signals were generated in the course of the same public campaign.

Consider the letter that Secretary of Education Linda McMahon sent to Harvard's president, Alan Garber, on May 5, 2025, which begins:

> The Federal Government has a sacred responsibility to be a wise and important steward of American taxpayer dollars.

> Harvard University, despite amassing a largely tax-free $53.2 billion dollar endowment (larger than the GDP of 100 countries), receives billions of dollars of taxpayer largess each year. Receiving such taxpayer funds is a privilege, not a right. Yet instead of using these funds to advance the education of its students, Harvard is engaging in a systemic pattern of violating federal law. Where do many of these "students" come from, who are they, how do they get into Harvard, or even into our country—and why is there so much HATE? These are questions that must be answered, among many more, but the biggest question of all is, why will Harvard not give straightforward answers to the American public?

McMahon's opening words reveal both a pivot away and a broadening out from the line of attack that the administration had taken against Harvard and other universities in previous weeks. That attack had mobilized charges of antisemitism on behalf of its quasi-fascist effort to intimidate and control institutions of higher learning. Partly because of the rise of Jewish voices against this tactic, the administration evidently saw fit to reframe the charge against Harvard for the purposes of the May 5 letter. The charge now became nothing less than "a systemic pattern of violating federal law."

And yet, in lieu of spelling out the meaning of this grave and sweeping allegation, McMahon raised a series of insinuating "questions" that suggest that something must be rotten in Harvard's attractiveness to foreign students. Her questions portended that shocking but predictable measure to suspend all visa interviews until the thought police could ramp up their surveillance capacity.

Most remarkable of all about McMahon's opening paragraph, however, is the question that comes last, after all the sanctimony ("sacred responsibility") and insinuations. It comes after a dash, and almost as an afterthought: "and why is there so much HATE?" There is much to say about this big little question and how it functions in McMahon's machinations against Harvard. The use of all caps is a gesture to the typographical style of the president, but more to the point, what is the sphere of reference? The question seems to imply something like: "Why is there so much HATE *there*?," at Harvard. But as posed, it seems to sound a more general and open kind of concern, like the puzzlement of someone for whom hostility and animus are just mysterious, alien forces in the world. Why can't we all just get along? What the world needs now is love and understanding. Why can't the hateful people at Harvard understand that? And why don't they answer a simple question when it is put to them? What are they hiding?

The irony implicit in an apparently simple question worded just this way, on this occasion, by such a person, is worth pausing over. First, although put to Harvard, the question is really—like the information that Harvard's endowment exceeds the GDP of 100 countries—intended for another audience, the world of social media where McMahon's letter was posted and reposted by the likes of Daniel Scavino, Trump's Deputy Chief of Staff, to cheering responses in the MAGA world. McMahon's "critique" of Harvard in these circles was called scathing, blistering, and, above all, well-deserved. Harvard, said the MAGA world, has had this coming for a long time. As for the Pollyanna-sounding tone of the question, some of the more tuned-in MAGA observers would certainly have relished the thought of such sanctimonious posturing, and indeed such false naïveté, coming from Linda McMahon. For the larger irony of this confrontation lies in the fact that McMahon, a cofounder of World Wrestling Entertainment, along with her indicted husband, Vince, should be Trump's point person on this matter in the first place. Indeed, the WWE is an enterprise that supplies multiple frames of reference for understanding the deeply cynical worldview shared by the McMahons and their intimate friend in the White House.

In 2013, Donald Trump was inducted into the WWE Hall of Fame. He was introduced that evening by Vince McMahon, with whom he had what he described in his acceptance speech as "an amazing relationship for many years" that, as he recalled wistfully, went back to WrestleMania IV in Atlantic City in 1988. Trump also recalled that, for WrestleMania XXIII in Detroit in 2007, he and McMahon had staged the "Battle of the Billionaires." This event turned on a "bet" about the outcome of a staged wrestling match, with the loser, in this case McMahon, getting his head shaved in the ring by the winner. A "struggling" McMahon was pinned down by a "referee," then covered with shaving cream and shorn by Trump with an electric razor. In claiming his place in the WWE Hall of Fame, Trump boasted, unsurprisingly, that WrestleMania XXIII had the largest pay-per-view audience in wrestling history. The video of the bizarre episode, with the billionaires scuffling awkwardly in expensive Italian suits, was in circulation before the 2016 election, and I remember thinking, foolishly, that if only more people saw it, Trump would be unelectable. If anything, it probably helped his cause.

In advance of WrestleMania VII, held at the Los Angeles Sports Arena in 1991, *Sports Illustrated* (March 25) produced a feature-length article about McMahon's transformative effect on professional wrestling. It began with a long verbatim quotation from the opening of what it called a "famous essay" by the great French critic Roland Barthes, "The World of Wrestling," the first piece in his 1957 collection *Mythologies*, probably the most widely read of his many books:

> The virtue of wrestling is that it is the spectacle of excess. Here we find a grandiloquence which must have been that of ancient theaters. [...] Even hidden in the most squalid Parisian halls, wrestling partakes of the nature of the great solar spectacles, Greek drama and bullfights: In both, a light without shadow generates an emotion without reserve.

And this, as *Sports Illustrated* staff writers put it, "brings us directly to WrestleMania VII. For in the latest of the World Wrestling Federation's annual editions of mad, mad, mad myths-on-a-mat, we will indeed experience another spectacle of excess." When the writers close their piece with a final tribute to McMahon by way of Barthes's suggestion that professional wrestling briefly "unveils the form of a justice which is at last intelligible," they miss or suppress the irony laced into Barthes's point about the kind of justice that stands thus revealed.

There is, however, a further connection between Barthes and Vince McMahon that the *Sports Illustrated* article did not spell out. One of Barthes's claims in "The World of Wrestling" was effectively the same one that the McMahons had used in their 1989 effort to reduce their tax burden by redefining what was then called the World Wrestling Federation as promoting a nonsport. They would later change the name to "World Wrestling Entertainment" to reflect this. Back in 1957, Barthes had been forceful in making what was for him a key distinction: "There are those who think that wrestling is an ignoble sport. It is not a sport; it is a spectacle." He had, in effect, provided an analysis of what is known in the WWE as "kayfabe," long before the term (possibly pig-Latin for "be fake") was adopted in the 1980s to name the governing convention of openly shared illusion that makes professional wrestling the kind of show it is.

Along with Trump, one of the other inductees into the WWE Hall of Fame that evening in 2013 was Trish Stratus, who had played her own part in the Linda McMahon story. Stratus, born Patricia Anne Stratigeas, is a glamorous Canadian wrestler who was enlisted for a series of episodes in the ring with

"Mr. McMahon" during her first year with the WWE. Perhaps the most notorious of these took place on May 3, 2001, when, having ostensibly returned to the ring to seek a public apology from McMahon for a prior humiliation (getting dunked in a tub of foul-smelling slop one week earlier), she was further humiliated when he, as the man who paid her salary, ordered her to crawl on all fours, bark like a dog, and then strip off her clothes. Further, the "angle" (WWE talk for storyline) included the insinuation of an affair between McMahon and Stratus, a suggestion planted two months earlier in an episode involving Linda McMahon herself. "Mr. McMahon," as he is called by the excited pay-per-view commentators, enters the ring to explain to the crowd that he recently attempted to divorce his wife. His declaration, however, caused a nervous breakdown, leaving her in a wheelchair and him feeling trapped in the marriage. He tells the crowd that he is resentful about this situation and thirsty for revenge. A seemingly catatonic Linda McMahon is then wheeled out by none other than Trish Stratus, and after some further taunting remarks, McMahon takes Stratus by the hand, leads her out from behind the wheelchair, and begins kissing and groping her in front of his wife.

Linda McMahon later separated from her husband. Vince himself would have to step down from his role running the WWE because of various scandals. (In the same week of May 2025, when the Trump administration suspended interviews for student visas, John Laurinaitis ["Johnny Ace"] settled with a plaintiff who accused him and Vince McMahon of sex trafficking and agreed to provide evidence against McMahon.) Linda McMahon, for her part, went into politics and entered the national spotlight when she was invited to speak on the final night of the 2024 GOP convention in Milwaukee.

And then, of course, Trump appointed her Secretary of Education. From that lofty post, after decades of orchestrating–indeed, participating in–the hate-filled scenarios of the WWE, she took it upon herself to pose the question "why is there so much HATE?" What's the relation between the faux-catatonic role Linda McMahon performs with Vince McMahon in their disturbing WWE skit and the faux-innocent role she plays with Trump in their confrontation with Harvard? What is the Linda McMahon "character" supposed to know and not know in each case? She is playing dumb in the wrestling ring. Is she also playing dumb in her role as Secretary of Education? How does one make sense of all this?

As a boy of twelve or so, I went to some wrestling matches in Asbury Park, New Jersey. One match involved one of the greats of that era,

Antonino Rocca, famous for having invented the flying dropkick. He autographed my program that night, a souvenir I kept for years. Rocca's tag-team partner was Bruno Sammartino, and these good guys ("faces") won their match against a couple of bad guys ("heels"), according to the records I have since checked. But what might I have understood by that victory? I know that I thought Rocco and Samartino were on the side of right. I know that I thought the flying dropkick was a thing of beauty. But I also remember a question being raised by an older friend about the legitimacy of the contest's outcome–something he had heard from one of his even older friends. He himself was uncertain, and so was I. When I encountered Roland Barthes's "The World of Wrestling" some fifteen years later in graduate school, I remember thinking that it all made sense, except for the part about the spectators never wondering if the contest was real or fake. We did wonder, but then we put that doubt behind us.

That is how I recall my experience of kayfabe in the moment, but these days I wonder more about how far kayfabe extends beyond the professional wrestling match. Was it kayfabe when Vince McMahon had Trish Stratus crawl and bark like a dog and strip off her clothes? Was it kayfabe when he and Trish Stratus made out in front of Linda McMahon in her wheelchair? Was it kayfabe when

Linda McMahon asked the president of Harvard, "why is there so much HATE?"?

Kayfabe blurs the boundary between the spontaneous and the staged because of the way it governs the rules of a game played on the border between the real and the fake: real and fake enmity, real and fake passion, real and fake violence, real and fake harm. The border is never certain, and it tends to shift as the game is played. When a wrestler named Rikishi sat on Trish Stratus to give her a "stinkface" during her early days in the ring, the move may have been agreed upon in advance but—how can I put this delicately—the contact was real enough. The episode in which she was humiliated by Vince McMahon was obviously pre-scripted. But, when ordered to do so, Trish Stratus really did crawl on all fours and bark and strip, and she did it for money. Linda McMahon herself may only have been playing the part of a traumatized wife when she was wheeled into the ring, but Vince McMahon was actually kissing and groping Trish Stratus before her very eyes.

Linda McMahon sermonizing Harvard about trading in hate, like the Trump-supporting Christians of the Esther Project accusing Jews of antisemitism, seems likewise to offer a troubling public spectacle made possible by dint of shared illusion. Indeed, the practice of kayfabe has become a distinguishing feature of Trumpian political spectacle more broadly.

Proposals to seize Greenland, annex Canada, reopen Alcatraz, investigate Bruce Springsteen and Beyoncé, run for a third term in office, introduce "permanent" tariffs, end habeas corpus, throw a military parade for his birthday—are these moves real or fake, silly distractions or genuine causes for concern? The question is posed on a daily basis in the broadcast, print, and net-based media.

Trump and his people also reinforce kayfabe with reality-defying spin that recodes events after the fact. Thus, when Trump said he would end the war in Ukraine "on day one," it turned out he was just exaggerating. Back in his first term, he wholeheartedly assured reporters at a news conference that he could see no reason Putin would be lying about intelligence reports, then explained the next day that he intended the opposite, that he simply misspoke. Or consider what he later labeled the "perfect phone call" he made to Volodymyr Zelensky offering arms for dirt on Hunter Biden, or the "perfect phone call" he made to Georgia Secretary of State Brad Raffensperger requesting exactly 11,780 votes to reverse the outcome of the election in that state (for which he was indicted in August 2023). It has long been recognized that the man who speaks endlessly of "fake news" trades in frauds and falsehoods to a degree unprecedented in the memory of any living American.

Others before me have commented on the Trump administration's relation to the WWE and to the practices of kayfabe. But the stakes have gone up now that Linda McMahon has become the point person for the Trump administration's efforts to bring universities into conformity with the agenda of the Heritage Foundation and Christopher Rufo. It is time to return to Roland Barthes. Since the surprising invocation of Barthes in that old *Sports Illustrated* piece on Vince McMahon, there does not, alas, seem to have been much interest in his essay "The World of Wrestling," yet two of his most salient points help to explain the world of Trumpism. The first has to do with his understanding of the disposition that wrestling cultivates in its spectators: "The public is completely uninterested in knowing whether the contest is rigged or not, and rightly so; it abandons itself to the primary virtue of the spectacle, which is to abolish all motives and all consequences; what matters is not what [the public] thinks but what it sees."

The "light without shadow generates emotion without reserve," and together this produces a spectacle without thought. This is the principle of kayfabe. There can be charges of foul play within the scenario of the wrestling match—just as there are charges of election fraud within the world of Trumpian politics—but these charges do not add up to the settled conclusion that the entire enterprise is trumped up.

A second point made by Barthes, which helps to clarify this one, turns on the relationship in wrestling among payback, rule-breaking, and a primordial idea of justice:

> But what wrestling is above all meant to portray is a purely moral concept: that of justice. The idea of "paying" is essential to wrestling, and the crowd's "Give it to him" means above all else "Make him pay." This is therefore, needless to say, an immanent justice. The baser the action of the "bastard," the more delighted the public is by the blow which he justly receives in return. If the villain—who is of course a coward—takes refuge behind the ropes, claiming unfairly to have a right to do so by a brazen mimicry, he is successfully pursued there and caught, and the crowd is jubilant at seeing the rules broken for the sake of a deserved punishment. [...] Naturally, it is the pattern of Justice which matters here, much more than its content; wrestling is above all a quantitative sequence of compensations (an eye for an eye, a tooth for a tooth). (Barthes, *Mythologies*, 20)

As in the world of wrestling, the trumped-up spectacle of justice on display in today's Washington is a stage-managed show of retribution and retaliation. In foreign and domestic affairs alike–from trade policy to the legitimacy of the 2020 election outcome–it is all about who has done what to whom, who has to be made to pay for it, and with what level of pain and suffering. And transgression beyond the actual rules governing the situation–in this case, the rule of law itself, brazenly, shamelessly–need not be thought of as a problem so long as the retaliation is successful and the "intelligible" spectacle of retributive justice is maintained.

The most irrelevant rule imaginable in both the MAGA world and that of the WWE would be a prohibition on retaliation as such. Unlike the world of wrestling, of course, the American legal system has rules prohibiting retaliation, though the Trump administration has flouted them in its vindictive attacks on institutions and persons alike. Trump's penchant for lawless retaliation got a major boost from MAGA allies in Congress when they buried in his "big beautiful bill" a poison pill that would limit the power of the federal judiciary to restrain executive orders found to be illegal or unconstitutional.

Barthes concludes his 1957 essay with a reflection on what happens when the show is over:

> When the hero or the villain of the drama, the man who was seen a few minutes earlier possessed by moral rage, magnified into a sort of metaphysical sign, leaves the wrestling hall, anonymous, carrying a small suitcase and arm-in-arm with his wife, no one can doubt that wrestling holds that power of transmutation which is common to Spectacle and to Religion Worship. (23)

This power of transmutation extends to our very understanding of how the world works. In the wrestler's grandiloquent gestures, Barthes suggests, causal relations achieve the timelessness of mathematical equations: "Each moment in wrestling is therefore like an algebra which simultaneously unveils the relation between a cause and its represented effect." But what of the effects of this "transmutation" itself? Do they end at the walls of the arena? Do they conclude when the show is over?

The various nonwrestling scenarios I began with—Vince McMahon humiliating Trish Stratus and then his wife, Trump and McMahon's battle of the billionaires—all represent McMahon's effort to make good, as it were, on his claim that his enterprise is not a sport but an entertainment. What further blurring of boundaries is involved when this expansive redefinition makes it possible for Linda and Vince McMahon to play, as it were, themselves?

How far can the magic algebra of cause and effect in Barthes's "World of Wrestling" be made to stretch? And what about the consequences beyond the even larger sphere of the MAGA circus—beyond the thrill of a Trump rally and the spin of Fox News? How long before it is widely understood that Trump's political and cultural populism has little or nothing to do with what is now called economic populism—policies that actually benefit working-class people? Might realities start to be clarified about who benefits from Trump's tax bill or who suffers from the cuts to programs for veterans and seniors, the rural and urban poor? About who eventually pays for Trump's politics of retaliation in everyday life? Will more Americans finally penetrate the massive kayfabe act that casts figures like Trump and Bannon as "men of the people" in the first place?

In October 2025, Trump announced that, as part of the nation's upcoming 250th anniversary celebrations, he had invited the Ultimate Fighting Championship to stage a match on Flag Day, June 14 (his eightieth birthday), "right at the White House grounds." In December, a tuxedo-clad Trump offered further details. The event, involving "the biggest fights they've ever had," would take place in the UFC's "Octagon Cage" before 6,000 spectators in a purpose-built arena, with 100,000 others watching on nearby screens: "There has never been anything like this, and there never will be anything like this." Who will rise to the task of explaining the full implications of this one-of-a-kind event? Barthes! Thou shouldst be living at this hour.

3

A "Broader Dynamic" in American Media

Fig. 5. John Cena about to "turn heel" against Cody Rhodes at the behest of Dwayne "The Rock" Johnson, April 2, 2025 (WWE). https://www.youtube.com/watch?v=mS8W6NY6QjQ

Roland Barthes's analysis of the world of wrestling as a spectacle without thought did not go so far as to imagine that such a world, through the expanded practice of corporatized kayfabe, could ultimately encompass the public life of an entire nation. In the grotesque and exaggerated gestures of this larger arena, as in Barthes's more restricted arena from the 1950s, the egregious displaces the normative. Satire, with its deep appreciation of irony and its capacity to make tone a medium of knowingness, has long been recognized as a key resource for dealing with monstrous developments of this kind. But how does satire manage in the face of the prophylactic ambiguities of kayfabe, the attempt to neutralize tone and destabilize irony itself? And what further mayhem follows when, in another twist, a kayfabe style of politics is supported by a crackdown on public media carried out in the name of free speech?

Barthes initially published the essays collected in *Mythologies* as part of a series of some fifty-three installments in *Les Lettres Nouvelles* from 1954 to 1956, an attempt to bring what he later called semiology, the analysis of sign systems, to the proliferating forms of postwar mass culture and media. But Barthes is not, alas, living at this hour, and we do not have anyone quite like him to decode the troubling signs of our moment through the medium of the literary essay. Perhaps we never did. In America we have not accorded our public intellectuals the same kind of respect that the French have accorded theirs. Or the same kind of attention: Barthes not only wrote about the young medium of television in his moment, he appeared on it often, with an impressive mix of cool and brio, though television never became his home medium. We have no Roland Barthes in contemporary America, but we do have some brilliant interpreters of contemporary politics and culture who have made the television medium their own.

One of them is Rachel Maddow of MSNBC. Stephen Bannon has gone on record on *War Room* (July 2021) claiming that MSNBC offered better news coverage than Fox News, and he singled out Maddow and her colleague Chris Hayes for special praise. Maddow has established her reputation on the basis of not only strong reporting and news analysis but also a capacity to provide longer historical perspectives on contemporary issues. She has written books on Spiro Agnew's attacks on news media in the 1970s, on American fascism in the 1920s, and on the history of Russia's dealings in oil and gas that begins with the discovery of "rock oil" in western Pennsylvania in 1859. A December 2025 podcast addressed the scandal of Japanese internments during World War II. One signature of her television reportage, her distinctive mode of decoding political culture, is to start a story off with some seemingly random event from the past and then "connect the dots," as her MSNBC promotional trailer puts it, to what's going on in the present. She might, for example, begin her coverage of a new authoritarian move in the MAGA world with a look back at the vast influence of Father Coughlin's quasi-fascist radio sermons in the 1930s. These longer historical trajectories lend Maddow's journalism a depth not readily available elsewhere in American mass media.

Bannon has praised Maddow's work, but he also may well recognize that her deliberate–sometimes too deliberate–style of presentation may not withstand the rage being generated on sites like *War Room*. As we have seen, Bannon himself describes his operation as programmatically stoking rage and retaliation to enable the resulting "angry voices" to be "weaponized." If "properly directed," he cautions, such voices "have latent political power." (Perhaps an example of an undirected angry voice would be the now largely forgotten Alex Jones, the TV snake-oil salesman who believed that the rage he whipped up on *Infowars* played a role in Trump's 2016 election victory; Jones even boasted that Trump called to thank him for his help.) In any case, a MAGA website is not a place for the open exchange of ideas. The liberal traditions of curated knowledge, reflective deliberation, and active sympathy often seem to prove no match for supercharged emotion leveraged for combat. This is one reason universities, founded on these same liberal traditions, are faring so poorly in the current struggle.

The crisis in America deepens every day in the midst of a public media environment turned warlike and cynical, the stuff of shared illusion. How does one engage a public discourse driven by weaponized anger? How does one gain rhetorical purchase? The history of rhetoric in the West, going back to crises of political culture in the ancient Athenian and Roman empires, would suggest that part of the answer lies in the realm of satire, which has grown in national importance over the past few years. There is more than one kind of satire in this tradition, but what its various forms have in common is a capacity for dealing with a world out of whack. Satirists have time-honored techniques for coping with bizarre public moments. They do not just unmask those responsible for delusional spectacle; they don their own masks to mock it. They fight dark emotion with levity—light emotion. Against a political community organized around anger, they convene one organized around laughter. Rather than mirroring rage with rage, they turn it into a joke.

Jokes mark the intersection between satire and comedy, but the overlap is only partial. Comedy and tragedy differ not just as laughter differs from tears, but also in their more general emphases, respectively, on community and isolation. Laughter and community both operate in satire as well, but in other ways. The joke in comedy tends to have a generalized field of reference, and, as cultural theorists Lauren Berlant and Sianne Ngai have noted, "it helps us test or figure out what it means to say 'us.'"

The satirist's joke, by contrast, is aimed at a specific public situation; it both presupposes an "us" and lends it solidarity. The satirist's specific form of community, that is, comes together with the force of a mutual recognition that occurs when a well-crafted punch line or well-timed gesture successfully targets an identifiable public situation. *Whew!* we say to ourselves, *I guess I'm not the only one who thought that was really crazy*.

To get a joke in any context is not only to know something but also to acknowledge that you know it. In the domain of satire, however, jokes often involve moments of acknowledgment that are conspicuously missing from the environment they lampoon. In "A Modest Proposal," his famous satire of British attitudes toward Irish Catholics in the early eighteenth century, Jonathan Swift adopted the mask of social engineer, or "projector," floating a new solution for the Irish population problem. His proposed scheme, published in the guise of a political pamphlet, is to serve up Irish babies for British consumption. The in-joke involves a send-up of the new discipline of "political arithmetic," which—like its successor discipline, political economy—tended to look to Ireland for its subject matter. Thomas Malthus's later treatise on population, for example, had Ireland squarely in view.

Swift's projector is a man so caught up in his numbers as to lose sight of the barbarism they imply:

> I do therefore humbly offer it to publick consideration, that of the hundred and twenty thousand children, already computed, twenty thousand may be reserved for breed, whereof only one fourth part to be males; which is more than we allow to sheep, black cattle, or swine, and my reason is, that these children are seldom the fruits of marriage, a circumstance not much regarded by our savages, therefore, one male will be sufficient to serve four females. That the remaining hundred thousand may, at a year old, be offered in sale to the persons of quality and fortune, through the kingdom; always advising the mother to let them suck plentifully in the last month, so as to render them plump, and fat for a good table. (Swift, *Essential Writings*, 297)

We do not know much about how Swift's pamphlet was received on its appearance in 1729—whether it is really true, as some have speculated, that there were contemporaries who took its proposal at face value. What can be said with some assurance is that for readers able to see what Swift was doing, the satire was as much an attack on the self-important institution of political arithmetic, in denial about its own implications, as on the colonial barbarism it served. Swift could be tough on other institutions too. There is no more trenchant satire of academics in the language than the one he produced about the academy on the floating island of Laputa in the third book of *Gulliver's Travels* (1726). It is populated with men so absent-minded that they require a personal "flapper" to snap them out of their speculative reveries with a good slap in the face, even as their neglected wives travel to the mainland below for their sexual gratification.

Swift's own models were classical—he sided with the ancients in the great quarrel between the ancients and the moderns—and this kind of humor at the expense of public institutions has long afforded satire the means to build solidarity out of society's radical middle. Yet the Trump administration's tactics pose special challenges for satire in our own moment. In a recent discussion of Trump and kayfabe, the brilliant young (and *literally* masked) Irish satirist who goes by the name of Blindboy Boatclub makes this point forcefully. "When you think of fascism," he says, "most of us, we have a clear idea of what fascism is ... Hitler, Franco, Mussolini," and "it's quite humorless": "it's 'solemnity, ... not being serious,' [but rather] the performance of seriousness" (https://www.youtube.com/shorts/58V91oKE0MQ, July 2025). Solemnity is easily punctured by humor, but the Trump administration is "not using solemnity."

Case in point: When this administration has people deported to Venezuela, "which is possibly illegal ... and clearly fascist," Blindboy notes, the White House "is posting comedy videos of these people being deported, but with the sound of their chains, and ... the official account labels it ASMR" (a video designed to calm anxieties). These videos, explains Blindboy, invite us "to engage in a kayfabe and the kayfabe ... is: 'this is all a joke.'" The official in charge of this is "not really bad"; he is just "a heel" in a wrestling storyline. Charlie Chaplin was able to puncture the solemnity of the Nazis in *The Great Dictator*, but in the case of the Trump administration, "you can't do any Charlie Chaplin on that, because they are making the joke first." Not only have they created a would-be prophylactic against satire, but they have also attempted to reverse satiric polarities: "they use memes and humor ... as a way to laugh at anyone who criticizes it." That doesn't mean that what they do is itself satire. After the second No Kings protests brought millions into the streets in October 2025, Trump posted an AI animated video of himself as a pilot wearing a crown and dumping tons of shit on protesters in New York City. Speaker of the House Michael Johnson tried to defend it as "satire," but the only thing that Trump's self-aggrandizing video has in common with Swift's skillful lampoons is the scatology.

As Swift showed, and as his Irish compatriot Blindboy Boatclub knows, the resources of actual satire to counter such moves are considerable, especially when it comes to the power of irony. Linda McMahon may have posed a kayfabe question about hate to Harvard, but that question is not unanswerable if the right tone can be struck. Though a master of tone and irony, Barthes himself did not identify as a satirist. But at this hour in America, satire, especially television satire, has emerged as a dominant mode for interpreting political culture in a way that answers to the darkness of the moment. There are many talented satirists working these days—including John Oliver, Jimmy Kimmel, Trevor Noah, Wanda Sykes, and Seth Meyers—but Jon Stewart and Stephen Colbert in particular have played an outsized cultural role during the rise of MAGA politics.

Like most great satirists before them, including Jonathan Swift, Colbert and Stewart hew to the moral and political center of the spectrum. Three centuries ago, Swift sent up partisanship itself in *Gulliver's Travels* with his mockery of Lilliputian factionalism—bitter disputes between the Big-Endians and the Little-Endians—whose fundamental disagreement was over how best to crack open a hard-boiled egg. Even though the egregious Donald Trump has come to preoccupy their ongoing attention, Colbert and Stewart make fun of both political parties from a moral middle ground. Colbert is a devout Catholic and devoted family man who makes no secret of either commitment. Stewart's own most high-profile activism includes work on behalf of American veterans and a nonpartisan campaign on behalf of responders to the World Trade Center attack whose disability compensation was being delayed by both Republicans and Democrats in Congress. The comic recognitions in which they both trade derive less from, say, attacking a certain political development as right-wing than from simply exposing it as weird, crazy, or hypocritical, or all of the above. This is why so much of their comedy depends on wordless mugging at an outlandish piece of video from the day's news.

The program that Jon Stewart hosted from 1999 to 2015, *The Daily Show*, airs on Comedy Central yet humorously introduces itself as "America's only source for news." *The Daily Show* established a new mode for satiric television commentary, a twist on the format of the late-night host's opening monologue, pioneered decades ago by the likes of Jack Paar and Johnny Carson on the long-running *Tonight Show* (begun in 1954). Stewart's innovation was to use his stand-up routine—performed at a desk, sitting down—to comment on video clips from the day's programming across the networks. After five-day-a-week broadcasts for sixteen years, Stewart left in 2015, thus missing much of the Trump era.

Stewart returned in early 2024 for one evening a week, and, relieved of the burden of nightly broadcasts, his decoding of American political culture has achieved a new level of brilliance. One of his most memorable recent performances came in an extended monologue on March 2, 2025, his first broadcast after Trump's attempt to humiliate Volodymyr Zelensky in their February 28 meeting in the Oval Office. Stewart began by addressing the question on everyone's mind about how to make sense of this bizarre episode. Perhaps taking a page from Barthes, he answered it by reference to the world of wrestling, but in a somewhat different vein.

Over a still image of Trump, Vance, and Zelensky in the Oval Office, Stewart addressed the general mystification as follows: "The best way I can explain what happened and show Americans how to process this new reality [is] with another shocking turn of events from this weekend." His inset screen then switches to ESPN video footage of a recent WWE wrestling event. With Dwayne "The Rock" Johnson in the ring looking on, a White man in wrestling trunks approaches a handsome blonde-haired man dressed in fancy street clothes, kicks him in the groin, then throws him to the ground. A woman from ESPN supplies the commentary: "On Saturday night from the elimination chamber, the WWE shocked the world when John Cena turned heel, joined The Rock, and attacked Cody Rhodes." Jon Stewart chimes in: "Now if that doesn't immediately explain to you our current geopolitical climate, then you must have grown out of watching wrestling through the normal course of aging."

Stewart's mock exegesis involves the specific wrestling angle of the "heel turn," the technical term for a plot twist in which one of the good guys ("faces") reverses roles. John Cena, Stewart explains, is indeed the "good guy of professional wrestling, Mr. Hustle, the Champ, the man who stood for everything, truth, justice, the guy who literally holds the record for the most Make-a-Wish Foundation meetings of all time." This is indeed the literal truth, and the number of wishes he has granted is more than 650. "People would get cancer," adds Stewart, "just to meet John Cena." In what Stewart calls his "metaphor," Cena is America, and although Stewart doesn't say so, Cena's gifts to Make-a-Wish might stand for, let's say, USAID around the world. Cody Rhodes is Stewart's Zelensky figure.

We are then shown what led to the groin kick. At the start of this episode, Dwayne "The Rock" Johnson enters the ring with Cody Rhodes, the reigning champ and also a "face" (good guy).

Johnson, who now owns the WWE, announces darkly to Rhodes: "I want your soul." Rhodes (Zelensky) replies that he has nothing to fear from the bigger and stronger Johnson (Stewart's Putin figure) because he has the backing of his trustworthy ally John Cena. Cena then enters the ring on cue and embraces Rhodes. But Johnson, standing behind Rhodes, catches Cena's eye and performs the cutthroat gesture. That's when Cena kicks Rhodes in the groin and throws him down.

The little allegory, based on a spectacle that had been staged over the same weekend, and broadcast on the Monday night show after the Zelensky meeting, is so elegant, and in its way so neat and tidy, that it almost seems (impossibly) to have been contrived in response to what all Americans saw happen in the White House the day before. It is a mark of the genius of Stewart and his team of writers that they are able to respond so aptly to the outlandish maneuvers of the second Trump administration. Though they don't say as much, they may have had some help from Fox News, whose headline coverage of the Oval Office meeting on *The Five* had already, apparently without irony, baked in the wrestling metaphor for their coverage: "Trump's Zelensky Smackdown." In any case, what Stewart and his team do every week is all the more impressive given the calculated acceleration of the news cycle—an explicit strategy of the forthright Steve Bannon—that has left so many wise heads spinning.

In concluding his decoding of the Oval Office meeting with Zelensky, Stewart goes on to spell out its implications with a guess about Trump's motives: "It was a 'heel turn' designed to create the alliance that Trump always wanted in the first place," the one with Putin's Russia, and ultimately against Europe and its political framework, the European Union. To support the point about Russia, Stewart offers a video sampling of Putin's comments on identity politics, sexual orientation policies, and transgender accommodations, commenting that Putin sounds like someone "primarying Marjorie Taylor Green from the right."

But the other side of the coin, the turn away from Europe, is just as crucial to Stewart's analysis, and one must, he says, give credit where credit is due: to "MAGA architect Steve Bannon," who has been "working to take out the EU for some time now." Stewart then shows Bannon speaking with his trademark candor about matters treated more circumspectly by others: "The beating heart of the globalist empire is in Brussels," Bannon declares in a 2018 video interview with *The Guardian*. "If I drive the stake through the heart of the vampire, the whole thing will start to dissipate. ... And that's literally when we take over the EU." Part of the brilliance of Stewart's satiric analysis is meeting Bannon's MAGA movement on its own terms. There is a certain fit between a kayfabe spectacle of raw, retributive, and often random justice—"emotion without reserve"—and a media platform like Steve Bannon's *War Room*. Mobilizing the one to expose the other is characteristic of Stewart's distinctive satiric art.

Stephen Colbert, who got his start on *The Daily Show*, has followed Stewart's innovation in the late-night monologue. On *The Colbert Report* ("Report," like "Colbert," pronounced as if it were French), his first solo show, Colbert presented himself in the persona of a vaguely pompous right-wing TV personality modeled to some extent on Bill O'Reilly, then host of *The O'Reilly Factor*. (O'Reilly's program was introduced every night, without irony, with the words: "The Number One show that dominates cable news.") Colbert's mockery of O'Reilly as an interview guest on O'Reilly's own show (November 7, 2007) remains one of the most hilarious episodes in recent American television history. Telling O'Reilly that he was the model for his own career, Colbert, in persona, mixed flattery and zingers until his host was utterly lost: "I wanna bring your message of love and peace to a younger audience ... [PAUSE] people in their sixties, people in their fifties, people who don't watch your show."

After a ten-year run on *The Colbert Report*, Colbert dropped his right-wing persona and replaced David Letterman on *The Late Show* in September 2015, just in time to cover the start of the primary season for the 2016 election. By the time Trump emerged from the pack of candidates in the Republican primary a few months later, Colbert had found his go-to subject matter and métier for years to come. No one over the course of this decade has captured Trump's character with more penetration or lampooned it with more skill. There was evidence that Colbert was getting under Trump's skin, but Trump continued to oblige him with fresh material—even or especially from 2021 to 2024, when Trump was out of office but much in the news—and Colbert and his writers knew how to turn it into effective satire. *The Late Show* became the most highly rated show in late-night broadcast television, and 2025 was shaping up to be a particularly good year for Colbert. In March he went to London to do a marathon interview with actor Gary Oldman that aired over four nights to rave reviews. In early July, *The Late Show* was nominated for an Emmy Award.

On July 17, 2025, not long after the Emmy nomination, Colbert announced that the CBS network was canceling his show, effective May 2026. CBS cited financial reasons, but the timing of this announcement raised questions. The decision came a week or so after CBS's parent company, Paramount, had decided to settle a suit brought against it by the Trump administration. Many legal observers thought the suit frivolous. And it was brought in the midst of an $8 billion deal, subject to approval by Trump's FCC, in which Paramount Global was acquired by Skydance Media. In his first monologue back from vacation, Colbert called the settlement a "big fat bribe." Two days later, on July 19, came the announcement of the show's termination. The following week Paramount announced that the sale to Skydance Media had gone through. Paramount Global, as it happens, also owns Comedy Central, *The Daily Show*'s network, and Stewart had already expressed fears for his own future even prior to the decision to terminate Colbert's show.

Were the reasons for Colbert's termination financial? No one doubts that broadcast television is in decline, late-night programming in particular. Yet days later when Fox News anchor Bill Hemmer asked Trump-appointed FCC Chairman Brendan Carr directly whether Trump had "anything to do with the cancellation of Stephen Colbert's show," Carr (as Hemmer himself pointed out) dodged the softball question by delivering a rather self-incriminating overview:

> What's important to keep in mind is a broader dynamic. When President Trump ran for reelection, he ran right at these legacy broadcast media outfits and the New York and Hollywood elites that are behind it, and he smashed the façade that these are gatekeepers that can control what Americans can think and what Americans can say. ... There's a lot of consequences that are flowing from President Trump deciding, "I'm not going to play by the rules of politicians in the past, and let these legacy outfits dictate the narratives and the terms of the debate." And he's succeeding. ... NPR has been defunded, PBS has been defunded, Colbert is getting canceled.

Soon, Trump himself weighed in. After crowing over Colbert's cancellation at CBS, Trump targeted both NBC and ABC: "Networks aren't allowed to be political pawns for the Democrat Party. It has become so outrageous that, in my opinion, their licenses could, and should, be revoked! MAGA."

One might speculate that this was just an idle threat—kayfabe. After all, Trump has been threatening to revoke network licenses since his first term in office. But the very threat of such a revocation is itself a form of control—an exercise of coercion not in keeping with the "rules" supported by the principle of press freedom in the First Amendment.

This is the key to understanding what Carr calls the "broader dynamic" in American media. Here, as usual, Trumpian rhetoric has turned the world upside down, suggesting that the legacy networks must, in the name of freedom, be checked by government coercion. Hence the pivotal importance of Carr's specific charge that the networks assume they can "control what Americans think and say." This "façade" must be smashed in the name of freedom, even if it means exercising government control over the press in violation of that most venerable of American rights.

Under this regime, laws and norms protecting press freedom can just, with a wave of the hand, be dismissed by the chairman of the FCC as "the rules of politicians in the past." Less than two months after Trump and Carr threatened the three major broadcast networks, ABC "indefinitely preempted" another late-night host, Jimmy Kimmel. Kimmel's offending monologue came in the wake of the fatal shooting on September 10, 2025, of right-wing political activist Charlie Kirk on a university campus in Utah. The ostensible reason for the cancellation was a comment not about Kirk's murder, which Kimmel had addressed respectfully, but about its politicization by a "MAGA gang desperately trying to characterize this kid who murdered Charlie Kirk as anything other than one of them and doing everything they can to score political points from it." Kimmel explicitly criticized those who celebrated Kirk's death, but he also added a comment about Trump's strange response when asked how he was doing after the shooting of his friend and supporter: "I think very good. And, by the way, right there you see all the trucks. They just started construction of the new ballroom for the White House, which is something they've been trying to get, as you know, for about 150 years. And it's going to be a beauty."

Kimmel then commented: "Yes, he's at the fourth stage of grief: construction. ... This is not how an adult grieves the murder of someone he called a friend. This is how a four-year-old mourns a goldfish." This follow-up probably offended the White House more than the comment about the MAGA spin on Kirk's assassin. As things fell out, the Walt Disney Corporation, which owns ABC, faced such consumer backlash that they reinstated Kimmel a week later, on September 22. Together with Harvard's continuing resistance to Trump's takeover efforts at about the same time, ABC's reversal sounded a note of hope that things might soon begin to turn around.

Questions of knowledge, information, and free speech link these attacks on the institutions of American media and the ongoing assault on higher learning. I have only half playfully turned to the world of wrestling, both the spectacle of kayfabe and the metaphor of the heel turn, for a pair of lenses to bring into focus the kind of decision making that underlies this campaign. Another such lens, however, is implicit in Trump's own metaphor of the networks as pawns for the Democrats. To understand how that one works means turning to a second commentary by Jon Stewart on Trump's Oval Office meeting with Zelensky.

4
A "Five-Dimensional" Game of Chess

Fig. 6. Michael de Adder, *Trump Is Not Playing 3-D Chess* (2025). cartoonstock.com.

Back in November 2015, when Steve Bannon conducted his series of three interviews with the man he hoped would bring victory for his Know-Nothing MAGA movement, Trump did not, like Bannon, pose as an enemy of the so-called intellectual elites that Bannon was fond of bashing, or as a critic of "immigrants." In fact, Trump specifically told Bannon on this occasion that he thought the country should find ways to keep the international students who managed to "do great" in our finest institutions of higher learning. Trump is rather more concerned to present himself as an eminent example of someone who managed to "do great" academically and continues to shine in all spheres of knowledge and intellect. How many times has he boasted about how much he knows about, say, science? He has declared himself not only part of the intellectual elite but also, notoriously and repeatedly since January 2018, a "stable genius."

That kind of boasting, to which we have become so inured over the past decade, was already fully on display in the 2015 interviews, when the claims Trump wanted to make for himself sometimes clashed with the picture Bannon wished to offer his listeners. In the November 3 interview, Bannon had disparaged his own education at Wharton, saying that all he had learned there was "supply and demand." In the November 19 interview, however, Trump crows about his academic success in the Ivy League:

> TRUMP: Numbers just came out in New Hampshire, numbers just came out, Fox

just announced numbers on other things and, you know, I'm leading on everything and leading not by a little bit but by a lot, but I have to say, you have to stop using the word "the intellectuals." I went to an Ivy League school. I was a very good student. I'm more of an intellectual than I think anybody–

BANNON: By the way, our audience here on *SiriusXM Patriot* and at Breitbart, where I say every day these working-class men and women, middle-class men and women are 10 times smarter than this intellectual group.

TRUMP: ... What can I tell you? Four months, five months. And I've been really very focused and when I focus, I focus. I've been watching these guys [on television]. They're wrong on everything. They are wrong so much. So don't call them the elite. Don't call them intellectuals. Call them establishment guys. You could say they're establishment because they've been there a long time. I think, "establishment," but you should never use the word "elite." I mean you should call me an intellectual. You shouldn't call them an intellectual.

While Bannon wants to castigate intellectuals, Trump still insists on being seen as one. And yet Bannon nonetheless finds a way to flatter Trump's intellectual pretensions, setting a template for the kind of toadyism that sadly continues to this day.

A few weeks after his brilliant commentary on Trump's Oval Office meeting with Zelensky in February 2025, Jon Stewart returned to that strange episode by referring to a game with rules very different from those of professional wrestling. Mocking the hyperbole with which right-wing news outlets celebrate the genius they claim to find in their superhero president, Stewart offered a quick sequence of four short video clips. It begins with TV judge Jeanine Pirro summing up the February 28 meeting on Fox News's *The Five*: "Zelensky is playing checkers," she declares, "while Trump is playing chess." In a second video, from a different episode, Fox host Laura Ingraham insists that Trump's strategic thinking amounts to "three-dimensional chess." In a third clip, a talking head in a suit proclaims: "four-dimensional chess!" Ultimately, as if not to be outdone, a final commenter takes the prize: "five-dimensional chess!" Stewart rounds off this comic bit with his own telling punch line. Posing a question about what Trump's so-called five-dimensional chess would even look like, he suddenly reaches under the desk and pulls out a chess board already set up for a game, white pieces on one side and black pieces on the other. "How would he do it?," Stewart wonders aloud, gazing at the board. And then, with a sweep of his arm, he clears off the black pieces: "First, we lose them for DEI ..."

Like Stewart's more elaborate bit about Trump and the world of wrestling, this simpler one debunking claims about Trump's tactical wizardry has stayed with me. But I have found myself wanting to take it in a different direction. Far from "five-dimensional chess," or what Steve Bannon in February 2025 called Trump's "outside the universe" thinking, Trump's characteristic moves, especially over the first six months of his second term, seem rather to have fallen into a certain predictable pattern, in keeping with his penchant for the dealmaker's fantasy of the "sure thing." His are the shortsighted decisions of a distracted, impulsive mind that latches on to the concept of a "win-either-way" proposition. This is not to be confused with the more familiar "win-win" deal enshrined in classical political economy, in which both sides benefit from a good bargain. The Trumpian idea of "win either way" is a dream of maximizing his own advantages irrespective of how the flipped coin lands—"heads I win, tails I win"—as if he had put his face on both sides of his new national 250th anniversary gold coin. The posture is not so much self-interested (in Adam Smith's sense of the term) as self-obsessed. Such an approach to decision making is so narrow that it misses the wider array of adverse outcomes. Even within a narrowly utilitarian calculus, what Trump is playing is not even checkers. It's more like a simplified fantasy of chess played on a single row, with just a king and a line of pawns.

For a case in point, consider again the meeting with Zelensky. Trump notoriously told him in the Oval Office that afternoon: "You don't have the cards right now." (True, it's a metaphor taken from yet a different kind of game, but we can work with it.) He would remind Zelensky of that admonition eight months later, in late November 2025, when the Russia-friendly "28-Point Peace Plan" was leaked. Implied but not stated in that initial announcement was that Trump was taking Zelensky's cards away in the very act of saying he lacked them. His words to Zelensky might be decoded this way: You can no longer stand up to Russia because we are defunding your effort to do so. Stewart may be right in speculating that the goal of this surprising move was to tip the outcome of the war, taking Russia's part against the European alliance and the European Union itself. If not dealt replacement "cards" by Europe, Zelensky would clearly have to capitulate to Putin.

Indeed, Trump's chief diplomatic efforts over the next months consisted primarily in consulting the Russians unilaterally about the terms on which they would be willing to stop the war. The end, with Russia appeased, would thus, as Stewart and others suggested, count as a win in Trump's mind. But there is another possibility, another outcome of the coin flip. What if the Europeans stepped up their levels of financial and military support for Ukraine? The war would be prolonged. More people would die. Russia would not be happy. But should all that come to pass, Trump could nonetheless turn to his MAGA constituency and declare that he had finally succeeded in forcing Europe to pay its fair share in defense spending. He would "win" either way.

Beyond the narrowed scope of the "heads I win" conceit, however, Trump's move against Zelensky has already had a range of adverse consequences. In taking the cards away from Zelensky and then humiliating him for not holding any, Trump took little account of what it really meant to strengthen Russia's hand as he did. Since that meeting in March 2025, Putin has made clear that what he imagines as a scenario in which "Russian wins" goes far beyond whatever Trump was able to conceive as a win for himself. Unable to acknowledge, perhaps even to see, the limits of his own one-dimensional chess move with Zelensky, Trump instead went public in late May with the report that "Putin has gone absolutely CRAZY!" And a few days later, Zelensky's devastating June 1 drone strikes on four Russian airbases showed that he had some cards left to play that Trump was evidently unaware of. In the meantime, the shortsighted move against Zelensky badly frayed the relationship between the United States and its European allies. So much for five-dimensional chess.

Trump's controversial tariff policy represents another example of this "heads I win, tails I win" tactic. On countless occasions, Trump has insisted that the goal of his tariffs is to bring manufacturing jobs back to America by inducing major corporations to set up shop here rather than abroad. As many sober economic analysts have noted, however, this can only be achieved if the tariffs are generally understood to be stable and long-lived, semipermanent. No major corporation would otherwise consider such a major course alteration, which would take years to carry out. In practice Trump's tariff policy has produced anything but a sense of long-term stability, because a new and different tariff scenario seems to appear every week. It's not just that tariff decisions look to be at the mercy of Trump's whims. They are also frequently motivated by little more than his beef du jour. What does a tariff on avocados or coffee beans have to do with American manufacturing?

Trump's announced willingness to seek negotiated tariff settlements would seem to suggest a very different set of goals from the fantasy of rebuilding American manufacturing. Trump might well emerge from a scenario of negotiated smaller tariffs by claiming new gains for federal coffers, and this might persuade him that with his tariff moves, as with his foreign policy moves, he wins either way. But tariff revenue, as we are constantly reminded by economic observers not employed by the Trump administration, is in fact a tax. It is borne initially by the American firms that import foreign goods and ultimately by the American citizens who consume them, and it is a regressive tax at that.

Moreover, readers who have followed the unfolding of Trump's tariff wars need little reminder of how contradictory and short-sighted his moves on this game board have proven to be. Each new announcement causes markets to bounce up and down. High tariffs on Brazil punish the opponents of strongman ex-President Jair Bolsonaro, and on Canada they punish its recognition of Palestinian statehood—political retaliation rather than economic calculation in both instances. By August 2025, prices were beginning to rise, and Federal Reserve Chair Jerome Powell cited the tariff policy as a reason not to lower interest rates, for which Trump has been menacingly clamoring. In the face of such uncertainty, much of the business world, both at home and abroad, has remained in wait-and-see mode. If there is one thing the business world doesn't like, as all the economists never tire of telling us, it is uncertainty.

All this was of course well known to anyone remotely keeping up with the news. Bound by the narrow conception of a "win either way," both of Trump's decisions failed to reflect even the two-dimensional thinking required for an actual chessboard. Trump remains blind, often willfully so, to a larger field of circumstances in which the adverse consequences of his impulsive maneuvers play out. This pattern extends across a range of other actions, such as the fatal rescission of congressional funding for critical foreign and domestic institutions, like USAID and the Corporation for Public Broadcasting, which announced its imminent closure in August 2025 and ceased operations in January 2026.

Consider in this light Trump's nomination of flagrantly incompetent loyalists to major cabinet positions. For the most part, these are people whose agenda, like Trump's, is in no way aligned with the mission of the departments they are supposed to be heading. Linda McMahon as Secretary of Education is not even the most egregious example of this kind of calculated mismatch. That honor probably falls either to Pete Hegseth, the Fox News weekend host appointed as Secretary of Defense, who by year's end was enmeshed in scandals over his attacks on nonmilitary maritime targets; or to Robert F. Kennedy, Jr., the medical conspiracist appointed as Secretary of Health and Human Services, whose handpicked panel of antivaxxers has revoked the long-standing Centers for Disease Control and Prevention (CDC) recommendation to administer the lifesaving hepatitis B vaccine to children. Matt Gaetz could well have earned the prize had his appointment as attorney general not been blocked, but the appointments of Attorney General Pam Bondi and Homeland Security Secretary Kristi Noem are both serious contenders.

Linda McMahon's role in the cabinet matters most to the fate of higher learning in America, as it faces threats unprecedented in our history. It is not just that she presides over the gutting of the Department of Education. She also, as became clear in the Trump administration's menacing of Harvard, emerged as point person for the siege being carried out on American universities. How, then, might Trump's brand of one-dimensional chess play out for this phase of his increasingly authoritarian strong-arming of American universities?

In an age when "flood the zone" is the byword of MAGA-driven change, it can be difficult to grasp the full range of measures that the Trump administration has taken against universities over the course of a single year. With some, of course, Trump has had the aid of a subservient, Republican-controlled Congress whose crowning achievement to date, the "One Big Beautiful Bill Act" (OBBBA) (P.L. 119-21) on taxing and spending, was signed into law on July

4, 2025. Several provisions buried in the statute target U.S. institutions of higher education. One is a further elevation of the federal tax rate on university endowments, by which some universities now face rates as high as eight percent—several times the previous levels. The bill also includes as many as eight major cuts to federal student loan programs, including a provision to end repayment plans such as SAVE (Saving on a Valuable Education). Student loans are capped at a lower ceiling and come with far less favorable interest rates and drastically shorter grace periods for beginning repayment.

The Trump administration did not need Congress to put into effect a new policy of screening the social media of foreign student visa applicants for content it deems politically objectionable. Since the criteria are so broad, it will fall to the official who happens to be investigating a given applicant to make the crucial determination, thus introducing a further level of uncertainty into the review process. The effect of this particular measure on the number of international students coming into this country is chilling: enrollments dropped 17 percent in the fall semester 2025. Trump's urging of this policy is easily enough explained in relation to his brand of one-dimensional chess.

Many international students will not make it through the process, and perhaps many more will refuse to submit themselves to it. There are other countries with good universities and high-quality degree programs across fields, and these are already attracting more and more applications. A reduction in international students is clearly something that Trump now thinks will count as a win in the eyes of Steve Bannon and the MAGA base. Unsubstantiated suspicion about the attractiveness of a university like Harvard to international students was very much at the heart of Linda McMahon's May 5, 2025, letter to Harvard asking why there is "so much HATE" and what all these international students might have to do with it.

But what about the students who do apply and manage to gain admission? On them, the Trump administration will have administered a political litmus test. If students abroad agree with the growing international consensus against both Israel's war in Gaza and unwavering U.S. support for it, best just to keep them out. But if they do come they need to be reminded that they will continue to be surveilled for "any indications of hostility toward the citizens, culture, government, institutions or founding principles of the United States." (In October, ICE purchased a new bot, formerly used in Israel, for surveillance of social media and moved rapidly toward building "a 24/7 social media surveillance team" to expedite deportations.) It must seem to Trump that he wins with the international students who never enroll in U.S. universities, and he wins with those who do. Heads I win, tails I win.

The damage done by the Trump administration's policy toward international students goes well beyond this restricted dimension. For a president obsessed with the balance of trade, he strangely has little appreciation for higher education as one of America's most reliably impressive exports. Our university system has been the envy of the world and has lured the best and brightest from countless nations to come to study in it. These students enrich the talent pool of our universities and bring diverse experiences in other languages and cultures that contribute enormously to the experiences of the rest of the student body, American students prominently among them.

What's more, many of these outstanding students have decided to remain in the country where they received this great education, bringing new talent and new perspectives to fields like science and engineering, law and medicine, and, within higher education itself, to teaching and research across all fields, including the humanities and social sciences. American strength across many fields derives in no small part from international human resources. Back in 2015, during his Breitbart interviews with Bannon, Trump seemed to understand this. The world-class reputation of American universities has been the accomplishment of many decades' work. The successful protocols for bringing in new talent and fresh perspectives from the international community have also evolved over time. In a field of play that is understood to include the vast advantages of this system, who in the world would want to take it down? Who else could imagine calling such a takedown a "win"?

Implicit in the picture I have sketched of the Trump administration are several disturbing ironies. Like other strongmen of the past and present, Trump has resorted to intimidation and bribery to gain unprecedented power. In his case, the ironies arise in how these tools are deployed. One can be found in the relationship between retaliation and whimsy in his short-term decision making. The wrestling world's practice of kayfabe offers a way of understanding this paradox—a wink at the crowd, a kick in the groin, and the show goes on. A second irony is how Trump's decision making hovers between impulse (whether whimsical or retaliatory or both) and calculation. Trump's impulses resolve themselves into recurring short-sighted bets that happen to strike his dealmaker's fancy as a sure thing, a win either way.

In Trump's attack on American higher education, however, there is a deeper irony, with origins in the moment when Steve Bannon and David Bossie went to Trump Tower in 2012 to see if Trump might be someone to lead what would become MAGA—their neo-Know-Nothing populist movement against the "globalist elites." At that point, Trump was a real estate magnate with a checkered history, the star of a reality TV show, and a man with a new penchant for generating false rumors about President Obama's birthplace. He had little or no sense of ideological orientation. Indeed, he had changed party affiliation several times over the previous dozen years: from Republican to Democrat in 2001, from Democrat back to Republican in 2009 (right after Obama's election), to "no party affiliation" in 2011, and then back to Republican in 2012. The Donald Trump whom Bannon and Bossie began recruiting that year and whose failing campaign they turned around in late 2016 was already a dealmaker playing one-dimensional chess, a man driven by whimsy and retaliation who used intimidation and money to get his way. But he was not a man with long-term objectives for a major political crusade. The third level of irony when it comes to understanding Trump lies in the interplay of the short-term instincts that have always been his own and the longer-term strategy that he willingly allowed to be foisted upon him.

Another way to put this is to say that the chessboard on which Trump is playing does in fact have a second dimension, with other chess pieces, but that is more important and more legible to the schemers behind his rise to power—Steve Bannon, David Bossie, Steven Miller, Russell Vought, the Heritage Foundation—than to Trump himself. It is true that Trump had some private beefs with universities: in his initial challenge to Columbia, the sum of government funding he threatened to withhold turned out to be exactly the sum he'd hoped to be paid by Columbia twenty-five years earlier in a failed deal that ended in sharp acrimony. His own foray into higher education, Trump University, was of course a humiliating failure. And Trump may well also be sensitive to the fact that he is no favorite on most American campuses. Still, the idea of going after the enrollment of international students does not seem to have been remotely on his radar until his recruitment to the war against "globalist elites" in Steve Bannon's America First crusade.

American universities have certainly had their own issues over the years; within higher education itself there have been ongoing debates about how to address them and, more important, how to address the problems that legitimately cause public concern: the high cost of tuition, the question of ideological bias, and the question of academic activism. Unsurprisingly, Trump, Bannon, and J. D. Vance (with the Heritage Foundation and Christopher Rufo in the background) have been stoking resentment against American universities and then trading on the results of their work. But do Americans really want to see our universities with diminished influence in the wider world, a provincialized student population, and a curriculum surveilled by the likes of Linda McMahon? Already in May 2025, in an AP-NORC poll, a substantial majority registered their disapproval of Trump's handling of higher education. Polls since then have confirmed this opinion as the current assault on universities came to be better understood for its role in the crusade to Make America Know-Nothing Again.

At the start of his second term in office, and within the narrow calculus of a one-dimensional chess game, Trump must have been persuaded by certain advisors that the student protests against U.S. support for Israel's war in Gaza made for another win-either-way scenario. His big move was to start mobilizing the charge of antisemitism to hold universities hostage to their needs for large-scale scientific research, especially medical research. (Universities with large medical schools have been particularly vulnerable because as of 2023, over half of federal funding for universities goes to the life sciences.) Any university that resists will necessarily find itself on the defensive, in need of millions of dollars to pay for protracted legal battles, and at risk of alienating pro-Israel major donors. If universities are embattled and weakened, Trump thinks he wins. But if they capitulate, as Columbia and Brown and Northwestern have done, they must cough up large settlement payments and accept forced changes to the way they go about their academic business—how they admit not only international students but all students, and how and what the students will be taught. Universities financially weakened or universities controlled and surveilled by government operatives—these are the alternative "wins" of Trump's campaign, all in behalf of an effort to Make America Know-Nothing Again.

This way lies madness. Whatever greatness America has, or had over the last century and a half, is at least partly dependent on the success of the great universities founded or transformed in the last quarter of the nineteenth century. Made possible by robust commitments of public and private funding, the eminence of the American university has also depended on two fundamental principles: academic freedom and diversity of background. The American Association of University Professors (AAUP) codified academic freedom in 1915 as a supreme value to protect speech and inquiry beyond the provisions of the First Amendment. In the summer of 2025, seven distinguished members of the Harvard faculty sent a letter to university President Alan Garber to urge a staunch defense of these norms. In January 2026, the outcome of Harvard's negotiations with the Trump administration was still in doubt. But even anti-DEI conservatives like Ross Douthat and Christopher Rufo have discussed in the *New York Times* (March 7, 2025) the notion that racial, ethnic, and gender diversity can have a specifically academic benefit.

Take away the principle of academic freedom and the drive to widen the horizon of diverse perspectives in the American university and you spell an end to the institution as we have known it. What greatness would be left in the society resulting from such moves is one of the questions I take up next.

5
A Time Without Universities?

Fig. 7. "'I did my own research,'" *Newsweek* (October 7, 2022).

A distinguished former university president of my acquaintance has shared with me a story she sometimes tells, knowing that it might be apocryphal, about a remark purportedly made by Hitler to "someone who dared warn him that purging the German universities of Jews and 'politically unreliable' members would mean the loss of his country's scientific preeminence." Hitler's response was: "Well, if that is what it takes to rid Germany of Jews, then we'll just have to do without science for a time." She, the former university president, goes on to pose the ironic question for this moment in U.S. history: "Can we do without universities for a time?"

The programmed unknowingness of the Trump era is perhaps most consequential for science and medicine. The withholding of billions in scientific funding for universities has already disrupted major research in both the physical and biological sciences. The National Institutes of Health terminated or froze 5,843 research grants in 2025; the National Science Foundation total was 1996. The American and global scientific communities have excoriated the Trump administration's cuts to initiatives aimed at studying climate change and policies designed to limit its damage. In their public appearances, administration officials in the relevant departments and agencies have developed the practice of giving a cagey answer to a straightforward question about the causes of climate disruption into a minor art form.

In the field of medicine, we should not have expected much from the second term of a president who, in his first term, recommended that Americans inject bleach into their veins as a remedy for the COVID-19 virus. And yet he has outdone himself. There is no question that the most egregious defiance of scientific knowledge by this administration so far has been the appointment of RFK Jr. as head of Health and Human Services (HHS)—part of a deal made for his public support of Trump at a crucial juncture in the 2024 presidential campaign. The playbook at HHS has been much the same as in other agencies under Trump. Cut funding, fire people who don't agree with you, hire those who do, no matter how absurd their credentials, and then push out a series of rapid decisions with disastrous consequences. In RFK Jr.'s case, these decisions typically both lack scientific foundation and carry life-and-death consequences for millions of Americans. In August 2025, to the astonishment of virtually the entire American medical establishment, RFK Jr. cut research for the development of mRNA vaccines, which, unlike bleach, probably saved millions of lives during the pandemic. In December, his hand-picked panel at the CDC overturned its long-standing policy to give infants the hepatitis B vaccination, which has been reported by the World Health Organization to induce immunity with a 95 percent success rate.

Long known as an antivaxxer, RFK Jr. published a solitary article linking vaccines to autism, "Deadly

Immunity," in *Rolling Stone* (July 14, 2005), based on research that *The Lancet* and the *British Medical Journal* later retracted as fraudulent. *Rolling Stone* itself retracted the piece, and *Salon* deleted it from its website, although its uncorrected version continued, and continues, to circulate on the internet. In April 2025, RFK Jr. publicly advised parents of newborns to "Do your own research" on vaccinations. The advice is to trust the internet, where, as he was well aware, his own erroneous and uncorrected version of "Deadly Immunity" can still be found, along with much other erroneous information. By implication, the sort of vetting that led to the retraction and removal of the article in the first place is to be discounted as interference by the people Steve Bannon calls "the clueless elites."

RFK Jr.'s sloganeering advice became a grotesquely comic meme during the COVID-19 era. For Halloween 2022, one kind of display for trick-or-treaters involved a skeleton or a gravestone bearing the words: "I did my own research." But the situation has only grown more challenging with the increasing deployment of various forms of AI, especially the new large language models (LLMs). Some observers wonder if these new technologies make the work of universities redundant or somehow beside the point. But the contrary argument is surely the stronger one: that the rise of LLMs makes the role of universities in producing and curating knowledge more crucial than ever. Scientific journals are flooded with fake papers. Carefully vetted technical work has issued from this same university system to raise worries about "model collapse" in the vast deployment of LLMs, and about threatened "hallucinations" in the information landscape that these programs are in the process of creating. Halloween revisited. Alarmingly but unsurprisingly (how often those adverbs appear together these days!), the big report released in May 2025 to much fanfare by RFK Jr.'s HHS proved on examination to include fake sources, some obviously generated by AI, as first reported by NOTUS (May 28).

Like Alex Jones, the snake oil huckster who lost $1.5 billion and his *Infowars* empire in a lawsuit over his claim that the 2012 Sandy Hook school shooting was a hoax, Steve Bannon was an early supporter of RFK Jr.'s bid for the presidency. After Trump made his deal with RFK Jr. and won the 2024 election, Bannon told the *Wall Street Journal* that he welcomed what he called the "fusion" between his MAGA movement and RFK Jr.'s MAHA (Make America Healthy Again) movement. Surely Bannon saw an ally who would bring in supporters Trump might otherwise lose—the Kennedy family had been synonymous with the Democratic Party for years—but also could advance his war to destabilize established systems of knowledge and information.

Like Bannon, RFK Jr. challenged existing institutional expertise in the name of a savvy populace capable of doing its own research. Like Bannon—but, in view of his family pedigree, even more preposterously—RFK Jr. now identifies as a "populist" seeking to "take this country back" from "elites and corporations," the combination "of state and corporate power that is strip-mining the middle class." His full-throated support for the U.S. withdrawal from the World Health Organization is a good instance of how his views also tally with Bannon's critique of the so-called globalists.

The alliance Bannon envisioned between MAGA and MAHA, along with the Heritage Foundation's efforts to take control of education, has done much to shape the second Trump administration's aggressive agenda. It goes without saying—though it is said every day—that the prosecution of this agenda poses unprecedented threats to the American political, ethical, and cultural fabric as we have known it. Moreover, on Bannon's explicit advice to "flood the zone" with frantic political activity, the outrageous moves come fast and furious. Some (deploying the National Guard in Los Angeles and Chicago, the ICE "Operation Metro Surge" in the Twin Cities of Minnesota, building a $300 million [then $400 million] ballroom for the White House) seem calculated to produce outrage, while others (the threats to prosecute Obama, James Comey, Letitia James, John Bolton, and Jerome Powell or the corrupt schemes involving Bitcoin) appear motivated by resentment, retaliation, or greed. It is hard to find words for some of the most extraordinary moves—not just the willingness to accept a massive luxury jet as an all-but-personal gift from the Qataris but also, in order to pay for its massive renovation, the clawing back of nearly a billion dollars (from the Pentagon's Sentinel program) initially intended to modernize aging nuclear missile silos in Minnesota.

Many of these developments seem without precedent, and may well be. Yet the ideological elements of the battle plan for Trump's gilded populism have been around for a while. Some date to the postwar era, including the Tea Party movement, launched by Newt Gingrich in the 1990s; the frontal attacks on America media by Richard Nixon and Spiro Agnew around 1970; and the anti-intellectualism of the attacks, mainly by Nixon and Joe McCarthy, on Adlai Stevenson in the 1950s. Universities faced political censorship during that same decade's McCarthy hearings, in which Trump's mentor Roy Cohn played so large a role. But there are much longer and deeper historical precedents.

I have argued throughout that certain other important reference points for the present moment lie in the Know-Nothing movement and its stoking of anti-immigrant sentiment in the 1850s. But the roots of some key tendencies now so egregiously evident in American politics go back even further—perhaps to the Founders, but certainly to the two-term presidency of Trump's personal hero, Andrew Jackson (1829–1837). The fact that Jackson came after the succession of Founder Presidents is only one of the reasons his presidency is sometimes taken to mark a new beginning for the young nation. Another is his strongman populism, which explains why Trump likes to pose next to the large portrait of Jackson that he installed in his redecoration of the newly gilded Oval Office.

At the beginning of Jackson's term, a young French aristocrat, Alexis de Tocqueville, arrived in America with his friend Gustave de Beaumont, to see for himself how democracy was faring here. Across Europe, Tocqueville witnessed an ongoing struggle in his time between democratic and antidemocratic forces. Although some of his own ancestors had been executed during the French Revolution, he expressed little doubt about which way things were headed. Tocqueville saw his moment in Europe as part of an irreversible process of democratization that had been ongoing for centuries, one that the French Revolution had both accelerated and set back but could not finally disrupt. His American quest was to see how democracy worked in a nation where it was not a late development but a founding principle. Tocqueville and Beaumont toured the country for nine months in 1831, then each wrote a book about what they saw and heard. Beaumont's was a provocative antislavery novel, *Marie, or Slavery in the United States* (1835). Tocqueville's book, *Democracy in America*, also published in 1835, remains one of the most important works ever written about American politics and a cornerstone of modern political thought.

Tocqueville met with President Jackson and treated him respectfully in his famous book, though he pointedly observed that the whole generation of leaders after that of the Founders represented a decline in the quality of American statesmen and did not exclude Jackson from that judgment. Never content to observe without analysis, Tocqueville took pains to explain the decline by pointing out that an urgent national challenge, like liberation from British tyranny or the making of a constitution, calls out talents that the ordinary business of politics does not. The problem of finding leaders fit to serve was not so severe in his eyes as to pose a serious threat to the great American experiment. One threat he did see as serious, however, he bequeathed to modern political thought as "the tyranny of the majority." Under this now-familiar rubric, Tocqueville addressed the problem of American populism.

The tyranny of the majority arises in part as a consequence of the crucial democratic institution of the vote. The side that loses a popular election or referendum must submit to the will of the side that wins. Tocqueville understood that the Framers of the Constitution were aware of this and commended them for taking measures—unpopular among Democrats today—like creation of the Senate Chamber, with two members per state, and the Electoral College. Other aspects of the problem are more nuanced and less easily remedied.

One subtler and more powerful manifestation of the tyranny of the majority shows in its effects on political expression in America. This deeper problem is not primarily about majoritarian-minoritarian relationships. In fact, it cannot be understood simply with regard to the people whose sovereignty makes democracy what it is; rather, it has to do with the relationship between the people and their leaders. One of Tocqueville's first encapsulations of the point comes in these simple observations: "I have heard Americans speak of their homeland. I have met with true patriotism among the people. I have often searched for it in vain among their leaders." This is one of Tocqueville's central puzzles, and he explicates it first by invoking a familiar picture of the monarch or emperor who dominates those he rules and then turning it upside down to challenge received assumptions about leadership and sovereignty: "This fact [about the American people and their leaders] is easily explained by analogy: despotism corrupts the person who submits to it far more than the person who imposes it. In absolute monarchies, the king often has great virtues, but the courtiers are always vile" (Tocqueville, *Democracy in America*, 301).

How this paradox works in practice is illustrated in Tocqueville's marvelous description of leaders in the act of flattering their patriotic sovereign, the American citizenry, with the rhetoric of populism:

> To be sure, courtiers in America do not say "Sire" and "Your Majesty," a great and capital difference. But they do speak constantly of their master's natural enlightenment. They do not offer prizes for the best answer to the question, "Which of the prince's virtues is most worthy of admiration?" for they are certain that he has all the virtues without having acquired them, indeed without wanting to acquire them. ... But in sacrificing their opinions to him, they prostitute themselves. Moralists and philosophers in America are not obliged to shroud their opinions in veils of allegory, but before venturing a nettlesome truth they say, "We know that the people

> to whom we speak are too far above human weaknesses ever to lose control of themselves. We would not speak thus were we not addressing men whose virtues and intelligence so far outshine all others as to render them alone worthy to remain free."
>
> Could Louis XIV's sycophants have been any more adept at flattering their master? (301)

Crucial here is the question of intention, for implicit in Tocqueville's "analogy" is the clear understanding that, like courtiers under an absolute monarch, politicians do not flatter their sovereign without ulterior motives. It is in this sense that they are said to be corrupt, to "prostitute themselves."

Ultimately, the aim of the courtier's sycophancy toward the king is to gain control over him, and the American leader's sycophancy toward the sovereign populace is likewise a power grab. According to Tocqueville's deeper analysis, a politician's motivated flattery of the sovereign populace threatens to put America on the road to a different kind of tyranny, the tyranny of the populist leader's form of rule. The bargain is deceptively simple. Trust me, the authoritarian populist says to the people—trust me to govern you as I please, for I alone truly understand your unalloyed greatness. The upshot is the revelation that the purest form of democracy has within it the possibility of turning democratic rule into its authoritarian opposite.

The application to our own moment hardly needs to be spelled out: Steve Bannon's all-power-to-the-people rhetoric and Trump's claim to "love the poorly educated" paved the way, it is now clear, for putting National Guardsmen and ICE agents on the streets of American cities. Despite flattering his MAGA followers' sense of victimhood with the promise to be their "retribution," Trump has used the increasingly unbridled power of the executive office to carry out intensely personal vendettas. Especially in this second term (to state what must now be utterly obvious even to a distant observer), he has also dressed his office—including his literal office in the White House—with the golden trappings of monarchy. Hence the strong purchase of "No Kings!"—one of the slogans of the opposition movement against Trump. And of course, sycophancy is itself now on almost daily display in the truly revolting spectacle of cabinet members kowtowing to Trump and corporate heads bearing gifts to the gilded Oval Office.

We should not at this dark hour forget the insight and the foresight of Tocqueville's brilliant dialectic, which shows how the tyranny of the majority in a democracy can revert to the very form of despotism it seeks to replace. Just pause to consider our state of affairs in the light of it: if you had set out to draw from scratch a fictional illustration of the problems Tocqueville saw in Jackson's America of the 1830s, you could scarcely have done it better than what the second Trump administration has delivered in the kayfabe spectacle of our nation's current political reality.

Surveying the American scene for a "counterweight" to some of the threats he saw as inherent in democratic populism, Tocqueville claimed to find it in a group that has not infrequently become the butt of American humor, the lawyers:

> The special knowledge that lawyers acquire through the study of law assures them of a distinctive rank in society. They constitute a kind of privileged class among the intelligent. The practice of their profession brings daily reminders of their superiority. They are masters of a body of knowledge that, while necessary, is not widely understood. (303)

John Stuart Mill, another leading founder of modern liberalism, reviewed *Democracy in America* at great length on the appearance of its English translation in 1836. Mill took special note of the importance of Tocqueville's discussion of the legal profession as a hedge against the dangerous tendencies he saw in full-on populism. Mill took the exception allowed for the role of lawyers as evidence of a larger acknowledgment "that there is no indisposition in the Many of the United States to pay deference to the opinions of an instructed class, where such a class exists, and where there are obvious signs by which it may be recognized" (Mill, "De Tocqueville on Democracy in America,"137).

Mill seized on this promising "lack of indisposition" as something that would augur well for America's future, imagining that one day the nation's increased economic prosperity might go far to solve the problem of producing such a "class." However, he had reservations about the lawyers' fitness for the large role they were being called upon to play. For Mill, the learning of this particular "instructed class," the legal profession's body of knowledge, was too technical, and too rote, to serve the needs of the young democracy:

> If the minds of lawyers were not, both in England and America, almost universally perverted by the barbarous system of technicalities—the opprobrium of human reason—which their youth is passed in committing to memory, and their manhood in administering,—we think with our author that they are the class in whom superiority of instruction, produced by superior

> study, would most easily obtain the stamp of general recognition. (137)

In Mill's counterfactual argument, if legal minds were not misshapen ("perverted") by their education and the practical necessities of their profession, they would have the profile requisite for saving America from Tocqueville's "tyranny of the majority."

For Mill, in other words, the American lawyer represents only a flawed incarnation of an "instructed class," being too caught up in both technicalities and practicalities. In the terms that we have learned to use partly from Mill himself, we would now say that an education that goes beyond the technical and the practical is "liberal": an education that opens a mind to free discussion and new ideas and helps it to become more deliberative in its habits, more analytic in its encounters with the world. Here then is another crucial link between the history of the early Republic and the current crisis, even as we look to jurists to protect what is left of the rule of law in America.

The 1830s in America, as surveyed by Tocqueville and Mill, was, with few exceptions, a time without universities. Mill cites verbatim Tocqueville's pithy observation: "Elementary instruction is within the reach of everybody: superior instruction is hardly attainable by any" (135). The vaunted American system of higher education—"superior instruction"—would not begin to take shape until a half-century later, after the Know-Nothing movement, after the Civil War. When this system did take shape, it incorporated many of Mill's ideas about what an educated citizen should look like. "Liberal arts" became the rubric under which countless small colleges were founded and promoted across America. Bard College, where, as I noted earlier, Kenneth Stern teaches students how to think about the problem of hate in the modern world, is one such institution.

Some colleges, like Yale (1887) and Rutgers (1924), became universities. And a liberal arts undergraduate curriculum was also installed at the heart of new research universities. Some were private institutions (like Johns Hopkins [1876], Stanford [1885], and Chicago [1891]) but many were indeed public and flourishing in states like Wisconsin (1848) and California (1865). In many of these new research environments, modeled in part on the German research university, the commitment to natural scientific discovery—*Naturwissenschaft*—was crucial to the mission. But even in the most "technical" and "practical" of these institutions of higher learning, the teaching of the liberal arts had its acknowledged importance: both MIT (1861) and Caltech (1891), for example, included the arts and humanities as a core piece of their undergraduate programs.

There are many ways the new system of American higher education answered Tocqueville's and Mill's worries about the seeds of tyranny that they detected in unalloyed democratic populism. Their own capacity for imagining such a system suffered from at least one severe limitation. Mill delivers the upshot of his counterfactual fantasy about what the lawyers could become if they were educated more liberally: "they would be the natural leaders of a people destitute of a leisured class." Repeatedly, Mill's remarks on liberal education fail to go beyond a residual investment in class thinking. He was one of the first thinkers to offer what Thorstein Veblen would later, with very different intent, call "the theory of the leisure class." Here is Mill's formulation:

> A leisured class would always possess a power sufficient not only to protect in themselves, but to encourage in others, the enjoyment of individuality of thought. ... A class composed of all the most cultivated intellects in the country; of those who, from their powers and their virtues, would command the respect of the people, even in combating their prejudices—such a class would be almost irresistible in its action on public opinion. In the existence of a leisured class, we see the great and

> salutary corrective of all the inconveniences to which democracy is liable. (137)

Mill's talk of the benefits of a leisured class, here and elsewhere, must have sounded a jarring note in contemporary American ears—and, let's face it, it still does today. A creature of the age of liberal reform in Britain, writing in the wake of Britain's Reform Act of 1832, he had not shaken the class system and the politics of inheritance championed by political thinkers like Edmund Burke. Thus, for all his praise of American democracy, Mill agrees with Tocqueville that America lags behind other nations in certain key respects: "in countries where there exist endowed institutions for education, and a numerous class possessed of hereditary leisure, there is a security, far greater than has ever existed in America, against the tyranny of public opinion over the individual mind" (137). Mill certainly seems here to have trouble imagining such a system of "endowed institutions for education" apart from "hereditary leisure"; presumably he can only conjure bastions of privilege like Oxford and Cambridge.

In his role as a public servant, though, Mill was more than a little capable of such imagination, and with impressively concrete results. In 1836, the very year he was writing his long review of Tocqueville, the new University of London opened its doors. The innovative approach of this institution was conceived on a plan drawn up ten years earlier by a group of utilitarian liberals including both Mill and his father, James Mill, and of course Jeremy Bentham, typically thought of as the founder of "the Godless Institution on Gower Street." The young Mill served on its first board of directors. This university rightly prides itself on its enviable record of "firsts." It was the first British university "to admit students regardless of their gender, race or religion, and to admit women to degree programmes." The overarching goal now avowed by the University of London is simply to expand "access to a wide range of academic opportunities."

That aspiration toward wider and wider student access came to be emulated in America with real success over time—uneven, to be sure, but real just the same. And in this aspiration too lies the key to uncoupling Mill's views about liberalism from his views about class. There remain traces of hereditary privilege in the American system, but they tend to benefit the oligarchical class Trump ultimately serves. "Legacy" admissions preference, which some universities had themselves been reducing, does not seem to be high on the list of charges brought by Linda McMahon's Department of Education. For a populist like Steve Bannon, for whom (for reasons that Tocqueville's and Mill's analyses make clear) an educated citizenry poses serious problems, there is every incentive to cast and castigate educated

Americans as a monolithic "class" of globalist elites. Yet the evidence to support such a view has been attenuated with every measure taken to broaden access to higher education. It dwindles every time a student gains admission as a first-generation college student or the horizon of higher education is expanded and transformed in other ways.

Mill and Tocqueville also make clear that an educational program grounded in classically liberal values should in principle foster the opposite of the groupthink characteristic of a particular "class." For Mill, after all, the tyranny of the majority also involves the tyranny of public opinion over the individual mind. Thinking of liberal education as the solution to Mill's problem returns us to the figure of Kenneth Stern at Bard College, the lawyer (as it happens) turned educator. As I noted earlier, Stern drafted the International Holocaust Remembrance Alliance's definition of antisemitism but now vehemently protests its weaponized deployment by the Trump administration to shut down debate on campus. Stern has not minced words. He sees in J. D. Vance's comments and in the Trump administration's actions an emulation of Viktor Orbán's tactics in Hungary: "Attacking liberal education and seeing it as the enemy."

No doubt agreeing with Mill and Tocqueville that liberal education should overcome groupthink in principle, Stern does not believe that colleges and universities are doing all they might to keep it robust:

> [They] may, abstractly, be doing a good job teaching students facts and theories associated with a wide range of academic disciplines. But they usually do not help students step back and think about how they think. That's a shame. Because if students were more aware of our innate tendencies, using brains developed over millennia to see ingroups and outgroups, they'd help produce graduates who crave complexity, and who think more clearly. (Stern, *The Conflict Over the Conflict*, 37)

Stern is not alone in this view, but certainly he himself, like many other American educators, is doing his part. He is director of the Bard Center for the Study of Hate, and his courses attempt to understand that complex problem with open discussion from a number of angles.

Stern's recent course for Bard's Lifetime Learning Center was titled "Hate: What and Why?" The questions to be addressed are available to the public:

> What is hate? What is it not?
>
> Is the potential for hate embedded in human psychology or is it learned?

> Under what conditions can people live together peacefully, and then turn on each other?
>
> How important is the media in teaching us to hate?
>
> What is the relationship of structural racism and individual prejudice?

Consider the contrast between Stern's thoughtful pedagogy on these very real questions and the snarky rhetorical question posed to Harvard by the former WWE President and performer who now serves as Secretary of Education: "Why is there so much HATE?" And then ask yourself: Could Stern's Bard College course make the ideological hit list for McMahon's Department of Education? For starters, it discusses antisemitism in relation to racism—even to "structural racism"—fast becoming one of the taboo topics of our Orwellian moment. Trump and McMahon haven't gotten to the liberal arts colleges like Bard yet, but only because they have begun with bigger game. If a course like Stern's were taught at a research university—Cornell, say, or Northwestern, or Virginia—it could appear prominently on the government's list of charges intended to justify the suspension of billions of dollars in scientific funding and even, in the case of Virginia, the ousting of the university president.

In the face of both the Trump administration's attacks on universities and RFK Jr.'s public undermining of medical science, most recent defenses of American higher education have focused on the question of scientific research. Such defenses are absolutely necessary in light of the urgent and palpable stakes. Government-imposed disruption of academic cancer research, for example, ought to raise a red flag for people everywhere. A modest little website launched by academic researchers—"What We'll Never Know"—has begun to spell out the scientific costs of some of the recent cuts to scientific work. There will be further such revelations about the consequences of these cuts as time goes on.

It is hard to say how much these disruptions bespeak an opposition to science itself, though Steve Bannon often uses the (for him) pejorative epithet "scientific" when he is lashing out at "globalist elites." Trump's Secretary of Education certainly cannot be counted among the staunchest supporters of academic science. Yet when the Trump administration makes its challenges to our universities, the charge is typically not that they are doing too much science and have to be stopped. The charges are more typically aimed at courses like Ken Stern's. "Structural racism," according to the

Trump administration, is not a concept that should be included in a course at Bard's Lifetime Learning Center, nor for that matter in a college curriculum of any kind. It reflects what they and their supporters like to call "liberal bias," which they insist must be stamped out at any cost.

This is not the place for a full stock-taking of the modern American university, which obviously still has a long way to go to realize its highest aspirations. It is not even clear that it had lately been heading in the right direction. The political theorist Wendy Brown has described a "hollowing out" of the liberal values that made "the North American twentieth century, for all its ghastly episodes and wrong turns, retroactively appear as something of a golden age for public higher education" (*Undoing the Demos*, 180). In this period, she writes, a college education "inclusive of the arts, letters, and sciences" became "the door through which descendants of workers, immigrants, and slaves entered onto the main stage of the society to whose wings they were historically consigned." Democracy itself demanded this. Citing Tocqueville by name on the dangers of a "citizenry left to its (manipulated) interests and passions," Brown argues that while democracy "may not demand universal political participation, ... it cannot survive the people's wholesale ignorance of the forces shaping their lives and limning their future." Hence her approval of the 1946 President's Commission, which declared "higher education ... an investment in a bulwark against garbled information, half-truths and untruths, against ignorance and intolerance" (28).

Brown makes clear, however, that public universities have done far more to educate a democratic citizenry than private ones, and she is aware that even public universities at their best had major blind spots ("aporias and occlusions"). They succeeded better in "articulating equality as an ideal" than in producing real social–or even educational–equality. More damningly, though, her view is retrospective. She sees the mid-twentieth-century liberal vision of the university as undergoing replacement by a neoliberal one in which all values are reduced to economic values, while the subject of education has shifted from the person and the citizen to the "job holder," understood as "human capital." Increasingly, "the market value of knowledge–its income-enhancing prospects for individuals and industry alike–is now understood as both its driving purpose and leading line of defense" (187). Brown knows that American higher education has long been vulnerable to such tendencies. One need only think of Thorstein Veblen's trenchant and far-sighted 1918 analysis of the influence of commercial corporations in academic affairs, *The Higher Learning in America*, a kind of sequel to his *Theory of the Leisure Class*. But many informed observers of American higher education would agree that universities have devolved in the ways that Brown has detailed since what she calls its heyday in the 1960s.

In the first conclusion I composed for this final chapter, I had been too defensive, insisting that, "unlike many of those that attack them, liberalism and its university are inherently and properly self-critical," and adding that although this can often seem like a weakness it is something to be cherished and not exploited. But a different and perhaps truer argument would urge that the liberal university has not been self-critical enough to evade the neoliberal takeover. Crucially, this takeover predates the anti-intellectual campaign of the MAGA movement: Brown's analysis of neoliberalism in higher education dates to 2015, just *before* Bannon and Trump teamed up to Make America Know-Nothing Again. Her critique, one among many that might be cited, would seem to imply more troubling answers to the question of why universities, with few exceptions, have defended themselves so ineptly in the current crisis.

To connect the willed ignorance of RFK Jr. with the targeting of courses like Kenneth Stern's is to see that, beyond academic science itself, the foundational liberalism of the modern university is also under attack in this moment. And it is being threatened for just the reasons that Tocqueville and Mill vividly anticipated. The recent academic coinage "authoritarian neoliberalism" might sound like a contradiction in terms, but it comes close to capturing something important about our moment, including the distinction between liberalism and neoliberalism. In these dark times, it is perhaps clearer than ever that the study of the liberal arts and sciences remains a crucial Tocquevillean "counterweight" both to populism and to the authoritarianism it can spawn. For the authoritarians themselves, this counterweight is just "liberal bias." Critiques of both liberalism and the institutions that embody it have often been harsh, by no means always unjust, and where they are just they must be heeded. But a year into the second Trump administration, we have begun to learn, in the starkest of terms, what it could look like to see our sites of knowledge production and liberal education brought under hostile control and transformed beyond recognition. It is time perhaps to ask ourselves: Can we once again imagine doing without universities for a time?

Acknowledgments

The satisfaction of getting this little book into public circulation has been deepened by the venue in which it now appears: a relaunch of the innovative pamphlet series founded years ago by my great colleague and dear friend, Marshall Sahlins (1930–2021), who figures prominently in this book's origins. But still more rewarding has been the experience of publishing it with his son, Peter Sahlins, whose energetic and expert contributions to whatever is good in it long ago went well beyond mere "editing." His interest in the project has been intellectual, political, personal, and most welcome. I thank him wholeheartedly for investments of many kinds and conversations in many places. Valuable critical input came from many other quarters as well, often

(I'm embarrassed to recall) after I would insist on reading a portion aloud in company as part of my effort to get the tone right. The incomplete roster includes Clara Badonsky (who also took on some copyediting), Homi Bhabha, Dipesh Chakrabarty, Carol Chandler, Kevin Chandler, Claire Connolly, Ian Duncan, Jeannie Essling, Ally Field, Colin Jones, Rashid Khalidi, Phil Lewis, Rochona Majumdar, Jo McDonagh, Dan Morgan, Ramona Nadaff, Paul O'Donovan, Don Randel, Joel Roszell, Kathleen Roszell, Jonathan Sachs, Laurie Shannon, Vincent Sherry, Eric Slauter, Jim Sparrow, Garrett Stewart, Alan Thomas, Joe Tomain, Domietta Torlasco, Cindy Wall, and Clair Wills. It was Bill Brown who read and shrewdly improved these pages from their beginnings in two pieces published last year in the *Los Angeles Review of Books* ("A Total Assault on the University," May 7, 2025; "A Trumped-up Spectacle," July 9, 2025). He also generously urged me to "to turn them into a small book." But it was my daughter, Catherine Chandler, who first challenged me to try to respond to the crisis unfolding early last year: "What are you yourself planning to do in the face of all this?" She has allowed writing to count as a form of doing, and helpfully counseled straightforwardness in executing it. Her brother, Michael, and his wife, Eleni Chandler Towns, have had their hands full with demanding public service jobs and two small children, but they have weighed in with timely advice and admonitions along the way, and I hope they forgive me for not heeding one of their warnings. My wife, Elizabeth O'Connor Chandler, read and listened to more of this than she should have had to, including parts that have since been discarded on her wise urging. No one has been more demanding about what this little project should be and do than my forever mentor Jerome McGann, who wrongly claims I never listen to him. Jerry's capacity to undertake both rigorous scholarship and engaged politics led Marshall to recruit him years ago for a pamphlet entitled *Are the Humanities Inconsequent?* (2009). This one is dedicated to him.

Editor's Note: The online edition of this essay (https://www.pricklyparadigm.com/the-know-nothing-campaign-against-higher-learning) includes embedded links to additional sources, images, and videos referenced throughout the text.

Further Reading

Abinder, Tyler. *Nativism and Slavery: The Northern Know Nothings and the Politics of the 1850s.* Oxford University Press, 1992.

Barthes, Roland. *Mythologies.* Trans. Richard Howard. Hill and Wang, 2012.

Berlant, Lauren, and Ngai, Sianne. "Comedy Has Issues." *Critical Inquiry* (Winter 2007): 43:2.

Brown, Wendy. *Undoing the Demos: Neoliberalism's Stealth Revolution.* Princeton University Press, 2017.

Colbrook, Claire. *Irony.* Routledge, 2004.

Field, Laura K. *Furious Minds: The Making of the MAGA New Right.* Princeton University Press, 2025.

Hofstadter, Richard. *Anti-Intellectualism in American Life, The Paranoid Style in American Politics, Uncollected Essays 1956–1965.* Ed. Sean Wilentz. Library of America, 2020.

Hutchins, Robert Maynard. *The Higher Learning in America.* Routledge, 1995.

Lear, Jonathan. *A Case for Irony.* Harvard University Press, 2014.

McLaughlin, Sarah. *Authoritarians in the Academy: How the Internationalization of Higher Education and Borderless Censorship Threaten Free Speech.* John Hopkins University Press, 2025.

Mill, John Stuart. "De Tocqueville on Democracy in America." *Essays on Politics and Society.* Volume 18. *Collected Works of John Stuart Mill.* Ed. John M. Robson. University of Toronto Press, 1977.

Mill, John Stuart. "The Spirit of the Age." In *The Spirit of the Age: Victorian Essays.* Ed. Gertrude Himmelfarb. Yale University Press, 2007.

O'Brien, Shannon Bow. *Donald Trump and the Kayfabe Presidency Professional Wrestling Rhetoric in the White House.* Palgrave, 2020.

Rorty, Richard. *Contingency, Irony, and Solidarity.* Cambridge University Press, 1989.

Roth, Michael S. *Beyond the University: Why Liberal Education Matters.* Yale University Press, 2015.

Stern, Kenneth. *The Conflict Over the Conflict: How the Israel/Palestine Campus Debate Is Eviscerating Academic Freedom.* New Jewish Press, 2020.

Swift, Jonathan. "A Modest Proposal." In *The Essential Writings of Jonathan Swift.* Ed. Claude Rawson and Ian Higgins. Norton, 2010.

Tocqueville, Alexis de. *Democracy in America.* Trans. Arthur Goldhammer. Library of America, 2004.

Veblen, Thorstein. *The Higher Learning in America: The Annotated Edition.* Ed. Richard F. Teichgraeber III. Johns Hopkins University Press, 2015.

Voss-Hubbard, Mark. *Beyond Party: Cultures of Antipartisanship in Northern Politics Before the Civil War.* Johns Hopkins University Press, 2002.

Also available from Prickly Paradigm Press:

1
Waiting for Foucault, Still
Marshall Sahlins

2
War of the Worlds: What about Peace?
Bruno Latour

3
Against Bosses, Against Oligarchies: A Conversation with Richard Rorty
Richard Rorty, Derek Nystrom, and Kent Puckett

4
The Secret Sins of Economics
Deirdre McCloskey

5
New Consensus for Old: Cultural Studies from Left to Right
Thomas Frank

6
Talking Politics: The Substance of Style from Abe to "W"
Michael Silverstein

7
Revolt of the Masscult
Chris Lehmann

8
The Companion Species Manifesto: Dogs, People, and Significant Otherness
Donna Haraway

9
9/12: New York After
Eliot Weinberger

10
On the Edges of Anthropology (Interviews)
James Clifford

11
The Thanksgiving Turkey Pardon, the Death of Teddy's Bear, and the Sovereign Exception of Guantánamo
Magnus Fiskesjö

12
The Root of Roots: Or, How Afro-American Anthropology Got its Start
Richard Price and Sally Price

13
What Happened to Art Criticism?
James Elkins

14
Fragments of an Anarchist Anthropology
David Graeber

15
Enemies of Promise: Publishing, Perishing, and the Eclipse of Scholarship
Lindsay Waters

16
The Empire's New Clothes: Paradigm Lost, and Regained
Harry Harootunian

17
Intellectual Complicity: The State and Its Destructions
Bruce Kapferer

18
The Hitman's Dilemma: Or, Business, Personal and Impersonal
Keith Hart

19
The Law in Shambles
Thomas Geoghegan

20

The Stock Ticker and the Superjumbo: How The Democrats Can Once Again Become America's Dominant Political Party
Rick Perlstein

21

Museum, Inc.: Inside the Global Art World
Paul Werner

22

Neo-Liberal Genetics: The Myths and Moral Tales of Evolutionary Psychology
Susan McKinnon

23

Phantom Calls: Race and the Globalization of the NBA
Grant Farred

24

The Turn of the Native
Eduardo Viveiros de Castro, Flávio Gordon, and Francisco Araújo

25

The American Game: Capitalism, Decolonization, World Domination, and Baseball
John D. Kelly

26

"Culture" and Culture: Traditional Knowledge and Intellectual Rights
Manuela Carneiro da Cunha

27

Reading Legitimation Crisis in Tehran: Iran and the Future of Liberalism
Danny Postel

28

Anti-Semitism and Islamophobia: Hatreds Old and New in Europe
Matti Bunzl

29

Neomedievalism, Neoconservatism, and the War on Terror
Bruce Holsinger

30

Understanding Media: A Popular Philosophy
Dominic Boyer

31

Pasta and Pizza
Franco La Cecla

32

The Western Illusion of Human Nature: With Reflections on the Long History of Hierarchy, Equality, and the Sublimation of Anarchy in the West, and Comparative Notes on Other Conceptions of the Human Condition
Marshall Sahlins

33

Time and Human Language Now
Jonathan Boyarin and Martin Land

34

American Counterinsurgency: Human Science and the Human Terrain
Roberto J. González

35

The Counter-Counterinsurgency Manual: Or, Notes on Demilitarizing American Society
Network of Concerned Anthropologists

36

Are the Humanities Inconsequent? Interpreting Marx's Riddle of the Dog
Jerome McGann

37
The Science of Passionate Interests: An Introduction to Gabriel Tarde's Economic Anthropology
Bruno Latour and Vincent Antonin Lépinay

38
Pacification and its Discontents
Kurt Jacobsen

39
An Anthropological Theory of the Corporation
Ira Bashkow

40
The Great Debate About Art
Roy Harris

41
The Inconstancy of the Indian Soul: The Encounter of Catholics and Cannibals in 16th-Century Brazil
Eduardo Viveiros de Castro

42
The Ecology of Others: Anthropology and the Question of Nature
Philippe Descola

43
Pastoral in Palestine
Neil Hertz

44
The Culture of Ethics
Franco La Cecla and Piero Zanini

45
2001 and Counting: Kubrick, Nietzsche, and Anthropology
Bruce Kapferer

46
Data: Now Bigger and Better!
Edited by Tom Boellstorff and Bill Maurer

47
Jean-Pierre Vernant: From the Maquis to the Polis
Jean-Pierre Vernant, edited and with preface by François Hartog

48
Confucius Institutes: Academic Malware
Marshall Sahlins

49
The Science of Myths and Vice Versa
Gregory Schrempp

50
Community of Scholars, Community of Teachers
Judith Shapiro

51
"Man—with Variations": Interviews with Franz Boas and Colleagues, 1937
Joseph Mitchell, edited and with an introduction by Robert Brightman

52
Making Trouble: Surrealism and the Human Sciences
Derek Sayer

53
Complicities: The People's Republic of China in Global Capitalism
Arif Dirlik

54
What the Foucault?
Marshall Sahlins

55
Populism Left and Right
Éric Fassin

56
Making Kin not Population
Edited by Adele E. Clarke
and Donna Haraway

57
The Gift Paradigm:
A Short Introduction to the
Anti-utilitarian Movement
in the Social Sciences
Alain Caillé

58
Kinds of Value:
An Experiment in Modal Anthropology
Paul Kockelman

59
The Jewish Question Again
Edited by Joyce Dalsheim
and Gregory Starrett

60
Presence and Social Obligation:
An Essay on the Share
James Ferguson

61
Can a Liberal Be a Chief?
Can a Chief Be a Liberal?
Some Thoughts on an Unfinished
Business of Colonialism
Olúfẹ́mi Táíwò

62
Subaltern Studies 2.0
Milinda Banerjee
and Jelle J.P. Wouters

63
Grievance: In Fragments
Grant Farred

64
Last Words:
Large Language Models
and the AI Apocalypse
Paul Kockelman

65
The Treadmill Affect:
Marxism, Subjectivity, and the Present
Benjamin Lee

67
How Do We Think About
Population in the Anthropocene?
Edited by Alison Bashford,
Duncan Kelly and David Nally